THE JOY OF SNACKS

A celebration of one of life's greatest pleasures, with recipes

LAURA GOODMAN

First published in 2022 by Headline Home
an imprint of Headline Publishing Group

First published in paperback in 2023

1

Cataloguing in Publication Data is available from the British Library

Paperback ISBN 978 1 4722 9157 8

Typeset in 9.75/15.25pt Versailles by Jouve (UK), Milton Keynes

Printed and bound in Great Britain by Clays Ltd, Elcograf S.p.A.

HEADLINE PUBLISHING GROUP
An Hachette UK Company
Carmelite House
50 Victoria Embankment
London EC4Y 0DZ

www.headline.co.uk
www.hachette.co.uk

'Deft storytelling, deep research and real wisdom
about how we actually eat'
Rachel Roddy, *Guardian* Books of the Year 2022

'Both joyous and useful'
India Knight, *The Times*

'As moreish as the snacks it celebrates, *The Joy of
Snacks* is a smart, funny and moving meditation on the
little things that make life great. I loved it.'
Ruby Tandoh

'Laura Goodman is a simply perfect food writer
and everything she does is a dream'
Ella Risbridger

'There are few food writers as witty and informed as
Laura, and I (unsurprisingly to me) devoured this book.'
Georgina Hayden

'It's so refreshing to read a cookbook that makes
me laugh! Laura does the near impossible;
her food and her good humour are as delicious
in real life as on the page.'
Alice Levine

'An utterly joyful read. I cannot think of a nicer
afternoon than to settle down with this book and
a variety of snacks alongside.'
Rukmini Iyer

'Naked, unashamed and witty, Laura Goodman
delights, tempts and insults our intestines with
raucous, dangerous and surprising suggestions'
Miriam Margolyes

Also by Laura Goodman

CARBS

For Rich, who is always ready to demolish a massive bag of crisps with me.

CONTENTS

WELCOME TO SNACKTOWN

We eat donuts with our coffee, pâté with our wine, nachos while we watch *Drag Race* and ice lollies in the garden. We eat crisps and dips whenever we get the chance, absolutely nonstop, you just try and stop us. Any and all events are snackworthy. This is how we punctuate our days with joy.

We eat snacks for lunch, snacks for dinner, and snacks at snacktime. We eat whimsically, by which I mean *according to our whims*, not *sitting cross-legged in a wildflower meadow surrounded by curious rabbits*. But it hasn't always been this way.

For a long time, we were encouraged to balance our meals carefully in order to keep hunger at bay until the next mealtime; the goal was to eliminate our unseemly inclination to snack. So, each January, we'd turn our attention to 'meal planning'. Everything in our lives would be more correct if only we would work harder on Sundays, stacking our fridges with boxes of boiled eggs, cooked couscous and cut cucumber, so that we might throw together a depressing meal at any moment.

Forbes magazine suggested we were clinging on to 'traditional eating patterns built around three "square", structured meals a day', but that gradually these 'had given way to modern eating styles characterized by frequent snacking'. And Bee Wilson wrote in the *Wall Street Journal:* 'There's still a lingering sense of moral disapproval about snacking, which is strange given that most of us snack more often than we brush our teeth.'

We are embracing snacks more all the time. But, of course, some of us have been snacking right all our lives. Nigella's silken midnight feasts have been taking place for as long as I can remember, even while her peers pointlessly filled vol-au-vent cases with prawns. And when my daughter Zipporah was a baby, one of the first questions she recognised (and responded enthusiastically to) was: 'Would you like a snack?'

If you want to snack well, the first step is admitting it.

I am never freer or happier to exist than in the moment I decide to go hell for leather on a bag of corn chips, forsaking my appetite for lunch. One thing that radically improved my first day back at the office post-lockdown was a chunk of tahini, fig and chocolate tiffin wrapped in greaseproof paper in my pocket. And the best thing I made in 2020 wasn't a meal; it was a warm, cheesy caramelised onion dip – deluxe and savoury in the extreme, devoured *communally* with hungry friends on a frosty Saturday afternoon before it all went wrong (you can find it in the dips chapter).

I have lovingly assembled this book to fill you up with snacking joy. I hope you'll snack on its essays, lists, thoughts, memories and claptraps as whimsically, unselfconsciously and wholeheartedly as possible – on the train, in your bed, at the park, while you cook, wherever you are, whatever time it is.

Are you going to ruin your dinner? Do you care? Are you a square? Will that couscous keep till tomorrow? Come on then; let's snack.

LIFE SNACKS I (USA)

I don't remember anything, unless you can tell me what I was eating while it happened. And I don't remember what I've eaten, unless there was a big feeling served alongside. Here is the first instalment of a patchy highlight reel, made of snacks.

- Generic red wine from Cupcake Vineyards and a box of Cheez-It Duoz next to a fledgling campfire in Yosemite after a long day of avoiding bears. Picture my bliss. I have no idea that later, in the dead of night, a family of raccoons will enter my tent. My snacks will be locked up elsewhere, but that won't stop those mad, creepy Cyril Sneer adversaries from leaving dusty footprints over my belongings (and my soul).

- A bag of blueberry cake donuts from a bakery in a strip mall near my auntie's house in Long Beach, with coffee, in her car.

- A large square slab of cheesecake from Canter's in West Hollywood after a day being busy and alone in LA.

- We hired a vehicle the size of a house in Texas in 2012. I wouldn't do that again, but the fact is that when another car went into the back of us within 30 minutes of leaving the Alamo office, it did not so much as rumple our bumper. We were flashing with invincibility as we remained within our fortress to eat a paper bag of tater tots from Keller's drive-thru.

- Bagels (pastrami, Swiss cheese and pickles) prepared by my husband, Rich, and taken up to the Griffith Observatory for a Friday night *La La Land* moment you hate to see.

- A Boston Creme donut from Kettle Glazed donuts in LA, smudges of chocolate glaze left clinging to the paper bag.

- Here's a triumph of international travel, and – as someone who left her engagement ring at gate four of Lanzarote airport – I don't have many of them. We made a detour to Russ & Daughters to get an airport bagel picnic before flying home from NYC, and handled our goodies with supreme care all the way to the gate. My bagel: pumpernickel, filled with smoked salmon and scallion cream cheese, wrapped in blue and white paper with the word PUMP scrawled on it. Also: a chunk of cinnamon babka, wrapped in clingfilm, bearing the word PIECE.

FOREVER FAVES

Crispy bits

I'm going to get into some classic snacks in this chapter, but before I do, I want to spend a bit of time thinking about one feature that ties so many of the great snacks together: crispness. Another Snacks Author™ might press on without acknowledging that if you fancy a snack, you could just buy yourself a bag of pickled onion Monster Munch and be done with it, but not this Snacks Author™, no way. This one likes to go deep, even if we just met. I love your top! How was your childhood? Let's talk crispy.

The sound of crispy

In a 2020 *Bon Appétit* article entitled 'There's an Entire Industry Dedicated to Making Foods Crispy, and It Is WILD', Alex Beggs put on a lab coat, assessed the copious research, felt fried chicken sandwiches betwixt her teeth, and headed to a mixing studio to meet the guy who recorded the Pringles sound library. But my main takeaway was per the heading: that crispy is an industry. There are scientists – many of them – devoted to 'making crispy crispier'.

The *Oxford Learner's Dictionary* has the definition of crispy as:
(of food) pleasantly hard and dry

But more scientific definitions refer to the sound the food makes when it shatters between your teeth. A journal article called 'Critical Evaluation of Crispy and Crunchy Textures' defines crispy as:

a dry rigid food which, when bitten with the incisors, fractures quickly, easily, and totally while emitting a relatively loud, high-pitched sound.

Dr Charles Spence, a Professor of Experimental Psychology at Oxford University, focuses on eating as a multisensory experience. In the *Adelaide Review*, he talked about sound as a 'powerful driver' for us in the enjoyment of food. And he pointed to the popularity of snack foods like biscuits, crisps and popcorn as evidence for the appeal of noisy food.

There was a t-shirt I wanted a few years ago by a Danish fashion label beloved of women my age that just said SNACK ATTACK three times across the front. The message is visceral, is it not? When I read the words I can hear a snack attack coming on. SNACK ATTACK SNACK ATTACK SNACK ATTACK. Foil packets, snatchy hands, puffy maize, furiously gnashing incisors.

In Spence's book *Gastrophysics*, he suggests that crispy's appeal might come down to it being a cue for freshness – like a crisp apple or lettuce leaf. But as far as snack foods go, it seems more likely that 'our strong attraction to fat' may be relevant: '. . . we all come to enjoy those foods that make more noise because they probably have more of the rewarding stuff in them than other, quieter foods.'

Crispy has been busy in recent years. Google's Ngram feature, which tracks the use of words over time across millions of books, shows a steep rise in use of the word crispy since 1980, getting steeper still around the turn of the millennium. Why? Most modern phenomena seem to be traceable to the rise of social media, and crispy foods do seem to make perfect snackable content – we can see crispy before we hear it. Or maybe it's just that the world is now so deeply troubling that we need to feel and hear food shattering between our teeth more often. We urgently need to nosh on joy. And crispy *is* joy, scientifically speaking. Studies have shown that we find crispy 'appealing', 'pleasurable' and 'fun'.

Crispy à la carte

The crispy foods that people lose their heads over on Instagram often come from the 'snacks' section of a restaurant's menu, especially in London – they're fritters, fries, bhajias and scratchings, resplendent from the fryer. This wasn't a menu section that really existed 15 years ago, and I'm a bit surprised to discover that I've been eating from London menus long enough to conduct this history lesson, but here we are – life just thunders along, until it doesn't, but anyway.

In 2011, some thirtysomething chefs known as the Young Turks, Isaac McHale and James Lowe, along with their front-of-house pioneer pals, Daniel Willis and Johnny Smith, started a residency upstairs at an east London pub otherwise known for its affiliation with Jack the Ripper.

They were serving cheffy food in a pubby pub and it was blowing even the most egregious high-profile food minds; 2011 was like that – we started to believe things could be different, or maybe it's just that I was 26. The offering at Upstairs at the Ten Bells was a set menu with four courses plus *snacks*.

They'd made a conscious choice to use their own terminology, and that included the word snack. Daniel Willis, who I met in ye olde Spitalfields way back then, told me recently: 'We were in the shadows of French cuisine and so "snack" was a way for us to reclaim "amuse bouche".' He summarises what they were doing at the Ten Bells: 'Ambitious food, tasting menu format, but in a dingy pub. And, obviously, very charming and casual service.' He jokes, but it's true. The service was key – they made fancy food feel like something we could have fun eating. Daniel helped, and so did the word snack.

The snack that was pictured alongside all the reviews and glossy magazine profiles was their buttermilk fried chicken in pine salt – these were perfectly craggy, golden nuggets served nuzzling pine leaves. They were crispy, as these restaurant snacks often are, because the point of them is to get you hyped for what lies ahead. To pounce on your mood and your teeth with pleasure and fun.

Sometimes menus have snack sections and sometimes they don't, but either way these snacks are not the same as starters – they're simple and shareable. I'm talking about little fried whitebait, calamari, mozzarella sticks, loaded potato skins – you know the guys, many of them are old friends. And I just want to dedicate a moment to a crispy centrepiece snack that does its job a little too well: the Blooming Onion at Outback Steakhouse.

This is an onion, cut to unfurl like a flower, battered generously and submerged in hot oil until every last petal is totally crisp. It sits in the middle of the table inducing mania – it's hard to believe no matter how many times you've seen it – and quickly renders everyone near it unable to eat their Outback Sirloin with Lobster and Mushroom Topping and Dressed Baked Potato. The Blooming Onion happens to be an onion, but it's really just a big, explosive, golden, inconceivable crispy, with a dip in the middle. The only thing that's as consummately crispy as this is the scraps on your chips. Both are wildly snackable.

Crispy at home

Discovering the wider crispy industry can shatter an illusion: we thought we were out here getting our crispy kicks according to our whims, but it turns out capitalism long-ago saw and raised our simple obsession with rigid, easy-to-fracture foods. What about in the private home, though? You return to pick at the bits left in the macaroni cheese dish just after declaring yourself done, and that's real. Those crispy bits really do happen to us, like magic, in our actual lives.

We, the home cooks, are also obsessed with making crispy crispier. Our tracksuits are our aprons and lab coats, our teeth are our Penetrometers and Texturometers (real machine names) and we induce the Maillard reaction every day like it's nothing (the chemical reaction that gives browned food flavour).

We have cute little passive aggressive fights at the table over crispy duck pancakes and the bottom of the paella (the *soccarat*! A crispy word if ever I heard one!). We hold the crispiest chips up to the light so that everyone can see what we're about to penetrate. We devote ourselves entirely to the skin of our pork belly, and routinely get burnt basting chickens and eggs. And we – busy though modern life indisputably is, all the research says so – will actually wait an extra 40 minutes to gratiné a Pyrex of cheesy food before we eat it. Lasagne tops are our jackpots.

Every Christmas, the media whips up a celebrity tête-à-tête about whose method creates the crispiest roast potatoes. At the climax of the year, as we all sit down to contemplate what really matters to us, the biggest names in food are finally, once and for all (until next year), pitted against each other in the ultimate test: crispy bits.

Nothing gets us going or keeps us coming back for more like crispy. In a 1990 article in the *Journal of Food Quality*, food scientist Alina Szczesniak wrote that crispness is a 'stimulant to active eating . . . It appears to hold a particular place in the basic psychology of appetite and hunger satiation, and encourages continuous eating. It is particularly well suited for consumption when the body activity is low, e.g. when reading or watching a movie or television.'

Active, continuous eating while watching TV, or as you and I know it: snacking.

The staggering potential of nachos

With a lot of foods that we've stolen from other cultures, we have at least a vague idea of how they started and how we might be corrupting them. For instance, we're aware of ongoing debates in the background of our lives about whether it's proper to add cream or white wine to a spaghetti bolognese, even if our family recipe contains mushrooms or Marmite. But nachos have travelled so far from where they began that most of us do not have a clue what a 'real' bowl (or basket? Or tray?) of nachos actually constitutes.

Most of us came to know nachos as the American cinema or ballpark dish of tortilla chips topped with: a half-arsed salsa, sour cream, beans, avocado, black olives, pickled jalapeños and cheese with so little cheese in it that it must legally be called 'nacho cheese flavoured sauce'. And if you're from the UK, your first nachos were probably a shadow of even this, compiled with Doritos, scepticism and restraint, which are three qualities that no one is looking for in their nachos.

Despite most of us starting our relationship with nachos the sad way, we still love them – because they are crisps with stuff on top, which makes them inherently great. This is a dish with more potential than a straight-A student, and almost as much as a slice of toast. If you have ever made nachos at home, you will know how thrilling it is to contemplate the prospects of your tortilla chips as you upend the bag into a bowl. Oh, the toppings you will scatter!

The real origin story of nachos takes place not in the Watford Cinema Park on the Kingsway North Orbital Road in Garston, but in 1940 in Piedras Negras, a city in the Mexican state of Coahuila, just over the Rio Grande from Texas. As the story goes, a regular customer from Eagle Pass in Texas arrived at the Victory Club in Piedras Negras out of hours with some pals and asked the maître d', Ignacio Anaya (whose nickname was Nacho), to fix them a snack. Nacho found some freshly fried corn tortillas and topped them with melted cheese and pickled jalapeños. He called it: Nacho's Special.

Is it good news that the original nachos only had three ingredients? Or is it actually woefully depressing to consider the miserable gubbins that British pubs are throwing on top of tortilla chips to make a dish they pass to the customer at a cost of £12.95, when it could all be so simple? You decide.

In 1995, to reclaim their joy, the people of Piedras Negras, together with the people of Eagle Pass over the bridge, launched Nacho Fest, which, every October, features record-breaking nachos, bulgogi nachos, caviar nachos, cheeseburger nachos, and jalapeño-eating contests. Festival guidelines state that nachos must contain three things – tortilla chips, cheese and a type of chilli – but otherwise, nacho artists should be free to express themselves. Compare and contrast to the guidelines provided by the Brotherhood and Sisterhood of Tarte Tatin in Lamotte-Beuvron, France. They state that any deviation from the original caramelised upside-down apple tart (apples, sugar, butter for the filling; flour, butter, egg for the pastry) must not under any circumstances be considered a Tarte Tatin. Your onion, beetroot and banana versions are tartes renversées (overturned tarts) at best.

Nachos represent adaptability, flexibility, change, possibility and fun, so they show up in places designed for fun, which is maybe why we love them even when they're bad. When I came to love LA's food scene it was because I felt hopped up on an experimental energy I was not feeling in London, where the rents are so high that every new idea must be a safe bet. At that time it seemed like you couldn't even be a restaurant in London if you didn't expose some brick and buy a joblot of Edison bulbs. I was so over it that my eyeballs were permanently at the back of my head, which was not comfortable. In 2016, I found LA's delicious, sunny freedom infectious and energising, and one of the best places to load up on it was via the nachos. The city of angels, strip malls and taco trucks gave me pig-ear nachos, lobster nachos, kale nachos and nachos in a bag. Plus, good old spray-cheese nachos and generously swagged 'classic' nachos too. It gave me juicy, zippy, delightful, blue-sky snacking life.

Please accept what follows as a topline summary of my lived nacho experience. Bad nachos, crab nachos, nachos that aren't nachos at all. What can I say? I play fast and loose. You should see my tarts.

Bad nachos, a haiku

Sigh. The naked chips.
I have run out of good times.
And I just started.

Crab nachos, a recipe

This is like a big, crabby, fiery, fresh salad with tortilla chips
as the leaves. All it requires is a bit of chopping and assem-
bly and your reward is a party in every damn mouthful, as
it should be.

Serves 2–4

¼ cucumber
3 tablespoons lime juice
½ teaspoon caster sugar
¼ red Romano pepper
4 little radishes
2 spring onions
¼ red onion
2 avocados
a handful of fresh coriander
125g sour cream
½–1 tablespoon chipotle in adobo paste
200g salted tortilla chips
100g white crab meat
2–3 tablespoons pickled jalapeños
limes
fine sea salt

1.   Get the ingredients ready to deploy, one at a time. First, the cucumber. Finely slice it into half-moons, and put them into a bowl with 2 tablespoons of the lime juice, the caster sugar and a pinch of salt. Toss, and leave.

2.   Slice the red pepper as finely as you can, along with the radishes.

3.   Finely chop both types of onion so they're sprinklable.

4.   Slice the avocados, as you like, and finely chop the coriander.

5.   To make the crema, mix the sour cream with 1 tablespoon of lime juice and the chipotle in adobo paste (starting with the smaller amount and adding more to taste).

6.   Tip the tortilla chips into a nice big rectangular dish like a roasting Pyrex or a deep brownie tray.

7.   Now scatter the crab, cucumber (leave behind the pickling liquid), red pepper, radishes, onions, avocado, pickled jalapeños and coriander over the chips, distributing them as evenly as you can. Take a good look. Do you want more of anything? Add it now.

8.   Drizzle the crema all over (use it all!).

9.   Serve with extra lime wedges and salt.

Crispy potato nachos, a dream

The chips best suited to wearing toppings in a nacho style are waffle fries, because of all that gorgeous surface area. But if you gently squash some baby potatoes before you fry them, you get something that might be better. Big, rugged, golden coins, with crispy nooks and scraps galore.

I got the idea for the recipe below from Matty Matheson's YouTube channel, which is my favourite quick televisual snack. He uses fingerling potatoes but it's not so easy to shop for those in the UK. To write this recipe, I used whichever small potatoes came in my vegetable box and tested it repeatedly with generic supermarket 'baby potatoes'.

In homage to Nacho, I topped the crispiest potatoes in the world with cheese sauce and pickled jalapeños to create a hybrid snack that's a spectacle of crispy excellence. I can't see why you wouldn't love it.

Serves 2–4

500g baby potatoes
60g Cheddar cheese, grated
½ teaspoon cornflour
85ml evaporated milk
2 tablespoons crushed tomatoes (or chopped tomatoes, crushed a bit before adding)
2 teaspoons Dijon mustard
a pinch of cayenne pepper
vegetable oil, for frying
flaky sea salt
1 spring onion, finely chopped
3 tablespoons roughly chopped pickled jalapeños

1. Boil the potatoes until completely soft but not falling apart – about 15 minutes once the water's boiling. Drain them and rest them on a chopping board when they're done.

2. Prepare some cheese sauce ingredients: mix the grated cheese and cornflour together in a bowl with a fork.

3. In a small pan off the heat, whisk together the evaporated milk, tinned tomatoes, mustard and cayenne, until even. Leave it there, poised and ready.

4. On a chopping board, flatten the potatoes one at a time with a masher – go as thin as you can without breaking them (though it's fine if some break).

5. In your widest frying pan, pour enough vegetable oil that it comes 1½cm up the sides of the pan, and turn the heat on.

6. When the oil's hot (you can use any stray potato in the masher to test the temperature), arrange the potatoes in an even layer and sprinkle with a big pinch of salt.

7. Fry the potatoes for about 10 minutes without touching them (you can use a fork to take a tentative peek underneath now and then), or until the underside has crisped right up and you can lift the potato in one without it breaking.

8. Turn and fry for 6–8 minutes on the other side, or until very, very crispy all over.

9. When the potatoes are done, lift them on to kitchen paper, then arrange them on a plate.

10. In the meantime, heat the milk mix over a low flame and when it's warm, whisk through the cheese and cornflour and keep heating and whisking until all the cheese is melted and the sauce is smooth and glossy. If it thickens up too much, loosen it off the heat with a splash more evaporated milk.

11. Pour the cheese sauce over the crispy potatoes.

12. Sprinkle over the spring onions and pickled jalapeños.

Once you pop

All hail the food that is named for being crisp (in the UK, at least). Time to make a little space, in fact, because we're going to tackle the elephant in the room. Crisps are snacks and snacks are crisps. Every other snack is just trying to be as good as crisps, which is a big and not necessarily savvy claim for what is still the beginning of a book containing 50-odd snack recipes.

If you've got friends coming over, you might make one or two of the recipes in this book: why not? I put a lot of effort into them. But whether you do or you don't, you'll serve crisps. I know you will. Potato chips, yes, but also puffs and curls and straws and balls. 'Crisps' made of beetroot or chickpeas or maize kernels or lentils or corn. You might help your pals wind down with some elementary cheese and onions, or you might prefer to demonstrate your social status with 'hummus crisps' whose bags have lots of green

on them and shout loudly about their questionable cre-
dentials. You may choose to wow your guests with a
limited edition kettle effort from the Co-op (they never
miss), or to take them on a sensory nostalgia trip via a buf-
fet of Skips, Space Raiders, Royster's and Wheat Crunchies.
Surprise them by demonstrating that M&S's Cheese Tasters are cheesier than Wotsits or blow their minds by
introducing them to McCoy's Muchos (the air pockets!
Astonishing!). Say 'I love you' with imported Cheetos; it's
the only way.

The sharing bags weigh 150g or thereabouts, and of course
that doesn't mean you're sharing them. In the UK, we are big-
time scoffers (technical term) (what else are we going to do
out here?), so we get through a good number of those bigger
bags without troubling ourselves to socialise. I don't know
about you, and I know that scoffing is complicated, but I love
to open them alone and never peg them back up. I feel free and
fantastic when I make a conscious decision to do that – I think
this is my version of sitting alone at a bar, drinking a Martini.
It is absolutely true that once you pop, you can't stop, and it
feels good to give in to that Pringly truth once in a while.

Modern food developers talk about the concept of a 'food
adventure' – we love to see the world via the crisp packet.
Crisps are part of being on holiday and they're also crucial
for finding the holiday in the everyday. You don't need me to
tell you this, because you're always thinking about the
moutarde Lay's you found at a baffling French bus station
and you like your paprika Crunchips washed down with a
Fanta Limone. I feel weak remembering the oregano Lay's

of Greece (the sweaty hike to the good beach), the garlic Munchitos of Spain (the pre-tapas tapas by the pool), and the Flamin' Hot Cheetos of the USA (the passenger seat of a hire car on a gaping freeway). In Japan, I made pilgrimages to snack heaven, 7-Eleven, where I loved seaweed crisps, soy sauce and mayo crisps, pickled plum crisps, pizza crisps and ponzu crisps. No one packs a packet with umami magic like Japan.

So there's the pursuit of adventure, and there's the pursuit of luxury, too: in the same way that we occasionally want to stay somewhere nicer than an Airbnb that smells faintly of drain, we occasionally want to bring home a giant bag of something souped up and truffly to distinguish the work day from the evening. A little hit of the outrageous, at a price we can just about afford, if we don't think about it too much or calculate our gross expenditure. And this is an area in which we buy in and we buy in again. We don't stop to check if we're being swizzed.

Not that crisps have to contain caviar to make our hearts skip a beat. Devoted snackers are always on the lookout for new flavours, but we're loyal to classics, too. There is not one thing from my childhood I remember more clearly than the way my mouth would water at the Tesco till when my mum paid for the salt and vinegar crisps. I knew crisps were special. Children know. It's no wonder that we still lose ourselves in the crackle of the packet, the oil on our fingertips, the first new-season crisp between our teeth. Crisps are wonderment. Crisps *deliver*. Good times are in the bag; you just have to break the seal.

Some crisps that have existed in the world

Raspberry bellini (Tyrells)
Raclette (Lay's)
Pecan Pie (Pringles)
Mint Mischief (Lay's)
Blueberry (Lay's)
Avocado salad (Cheetos)
Kebab and onion (Crunchips)
Vanilla ice cream (Monster Munch)
Salted caramel and double cream (Kettle Chips)
Labneh and mint (Lays)

Crispy curry chickpeas

Just as I, a millennial, am not ashamed of spending too much money on oat lattes (a source of many of the golden joy coins in my metaphorical treasure chest), I love chickpeas. They don't always get a fair crack; for instance, I once attended a vegan taco pop-up where the proprietors used a chickpea slur as their USP ('not a chickpea in sight'), which I felt was way off the mark.

I love the chickpea's life-saving versatility. Kids love hummus and granddads do, too, if they're brave enough to try. In these uncertain times, you can never have too many ways to use your chickpeas.

So here they are, made crisp and snackable, and smothered with flavour. The recipe makes a bowlful for two people to pick at while they wait for dinner.

Serves 2

1 x 400g tin of chickpeas
1 tablespoon olive oil
½ teaspoon fine sea salt
2 teaspoons curry powder
flaky sea salt
½ lemon

1. Preheat your oven to 200°C/180C fan/gas 6.

2. Drain the chickpeas well, then tip them into the middle of a clean, dry tea towel. Roll them around under your hands until they're completely dry.

3. In the rolling process, some of the chickpeas' skins will loosen. Don't go mad trying to remove every last sheath, but help along the ones that are on their way.

4. Tip the chickpeas into a roasting tray and toss with the olive oil and fine sea salt.

5. Bake for about 30 minutes, shuffling them around every 10 minutes so they cook evenly, until they're crispy.

6. Toss them with the curry powder, a big pinch of flaky sea salt and a squeeze of lemon. Get 'em while they're hot.

CAMPOP (The Campaign for Real Popcorn)

The bagged popcorn you can get as part of a meal deal is a health fad in disguise and it doesn't taste good. On the face of it, it's a chance to team your sandwich with a wacky savoury snack. But the reality is cardboardy. These popcorns yield about 3% of the salty joy they promise on their jolly bags.

But hot popcorn tossed in so much butter or oil that it's slippery – now there's a snack made in heaven. And in this state, popcorn can seize whatever flavourings you throw at it, and then it really pops.

That's the popcorn I want for you when you're having a low-key weekend; you only need a few minutes to surprise the people you love when they wake up from their nap. This is how you have an at-home cinema experience so cosy you kick your legs out with glee, sending popcorn shooting across the room. Good popcorn is lovely with wine, cocktails, hot chocolate, soda or tea – that's versatility. A bag of kernels costs £1.25 and equipment-wise, all you need is a saucepan with a lid. It's a no-brainer! Just watch your blankets for grease.

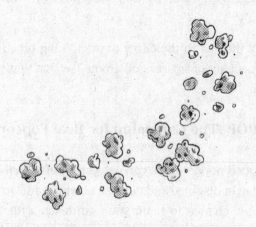

Popcorn on the hob

(I'm sorry I can't remember where I picked up the 4-kernel technique, but it really helped me put a stop to both burnt bits and unpopped bits.)

1. Put 2 tablespoons of groundnut or coconut oil into a wide pan with a lid, along with 4 popcorn kernels.

2. Put the lid on the pan, turn the heat up to medium and wait for all 4 kernels to pop.

3. Turn the heat off, add 100g of kernels to the pan and swirl it so that they're all coated with oil.

4. Count to 30, then put the lid on and turn the heat up to medium.

5. When the corn starts popping, move the lid so it sits slightly ajar.

6. When the popping slows and there are about 3 seconds between each pop, you're done – turn the heat off.

What's your flavour? (Tell me what's your flavour.)

Paprika and 'cheese'

Melt 60g of salted butter (or vegan alternative) in a small pan with 3 tablespoons of nutritional yeast flakes (the 'cheese') and ½ a teaspoon of hot smoked paprika. Add to the popcorn pan, put the lid on and shake.

Truffle and Parmesan

Add 4 tablespoons of white truffle oil and 55g of finely grated Parmesan to the pan, put the lid on and shake.

Brown sugar and cinnamon

Melt 60g of salted butter (or vegan alternative) in a small pan with 2 tablespoons of brown sugar and 1 teaspoon of cinnamon. So as not to burn the cinnamon, drizzle this on the popcorn once it's in the bowl rather than while it's in the pan.

Accept all cookies? Nah, mate

When I see a cookie and decide to buy it, I know what I expect from it. It's not that there is only one way for me to enjoy a cookie, it's that I require a cookie baker to have committed to the direction they chose. So, if the cookie before me is a wide, flat disc, then yes, I do need it to be crisp at the edges and chewy everywhere else. But let this cookie be that and more – let the baker have understood that what they're producing is an important artefact of wonder, so they have browned the butter and doubled the vanilla accordingly. If the café taking my money claims its cookie is salty, let there be flaky salt on top of an already salted butter dough. And if a cookie is meant to be 'double chocolate' then let me be absolutely clear: it won't be enough that it's brown in colour – it must have abundant chunks. I'm handing my money over, and in return, I need you to have tried.

I don't think that's a lot to ask, but have you noticed how bad people are at their jobs sometimes? I added that 'sometimes' to make me seem more reasonable than I am, but have you noticed how bad people are at their jobs? The truth is, I've never bought as many disappointing anythings as I have cookies. Usually: they're dry and hard, and they don't have enough chocolate in them.

Cookies I have loved include: warm, crumbly ones brought to my table when my lunch was delayed, a big, malty one in a restaurant where it was the only dessert on the menu (very cool move), sweet ones with white chocolate in them, chic ones with tahini in them, cookies with felicitations iced on top, cookies with Kinder Buenos pressed on top, commiseration cookies, party cookies, skillet cookies, warm ones, cakey ones, chewy ones, ones that are really chocolate shortbread, a praline one that came with free soft serve because the waiter didn't want to see me eat it without, even though it was breakfast time. There is never only one way.

There is only really one way I make them at home, though. And that's *the consummate chocolate chip cookie, revisited* by Deb Perelman aka Smitten Kitchen. This is as close to an ideal classic cookie as I can imagine: wide, with crunchy edges and chewy or gooey insides (depending on how recently it was baked). I keep the dough balled up in the freezer, ready to go into the oven at a moment's notice. When my uncle-in-law ate one, he asked if there was 'any cookie in this chocolate', and Perelman says her father-in-law made almost exactly the same joke. Maybe my ideal cookie is one that shocks in-laws.

When my daughter was very little, some women from the NCT group came round, one of whom I suspected I loved and one of whom I suspected I loathed. The woman I suspected I loathed demanded I make lunch, and I was a shadow of myself, so I agreed, and I also said I'd bake some of the precious cookie dough in the freezer. And do you know what she brought with her? She brought a packet of cookies. And do you know what she ate while she was here? She ate the tuna melt she'd demanded and then she ate one of the cookies she'd brought, and ignored mine. She was a bad cookie. The woman I suspected I loved ate only my cookies and then she cleared up and got everyone out of the house as soon as she realised my child was covered in vomit. A good cookie.

In Deb Perelman's recipe, she talks about 'magnificence on a plate'. A good cookie commands the plate, whether it's small or large, whether you can see a little of the plate behind it, or a lot. It's the singleness and singularity of the cookie, its completeness, its circularity, the way it holds all that it is inside of it. We accept it for what it is, unless it's bad.

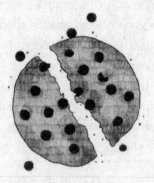

A schmear campaign

What are shop-bought bagels anyway? Are they a more shapely way to enjoy toast? Or are they a marketing ploy designed to sell bad bread by making us feel closer to glamorous New York City?

I grew up on real bagels from the Jewish deli – not in New York, but in suburban north-west London. Fancy London restaurants now tend to present their bagel platters as coming with a 'schmear', 'lox' and 'scallions' because they'd rather align themselves with the Big Apple and comedians and celebrity delis than with the epically grey and bollardy A41, but in Hendon, Edgware, Golders Green, you can find chewy, blistered rings that do not need to see a toaster until day three. (These are the same bakeries that supply the fancy restaurants, by the way.) And while you're there, you can pick up a babka, which you've heard about (a twisted, sweet chocolate loaf) and a bag of rugelach which you might not have (crescent-shaped chocolate pastries).

Growing up in a largely brunchless society, my family's Sunday ritual involved topping each bagel half with cream cheese and smoked salmon, or chopped liver, or egg and onion, and arranging them open-faced on big plates so everyone could take what they wanted, with a fish ball on the side.

Later, when my friends and I were very cool dudes who liked to arrive at nights out in the West End by car, my friend Joanna would drive her Ford KA to Carmelli's at 3 a.m. so we could get pre-filled, clingfilmed bagels for the road. And I've got to tell you: you cannot get close to the barefaced midnight joy of tearing at one of those be-salmoned beasts with your teeth via the supermarket baked-goods aisle.

I am thrilled to announce, though, that there is a use for your round, holey bread snacks: pizza bagels. These supermarket 'bagels' are profoundly lacking in so many ways: texture, flavour, authenticity, overall satisfaction, to name a few. But what I will say for them is this: they're bouncy. Which means they form a good base for lots of cheese and sauce (better than any pre-made pizza base I've ever tried), especially if you arrange things Sicilian-style (mozzarella *under* the sauce). Almost-instant pizza, what's not to like? It's two classic snacks in one.

You could top these further – with pepperoni, peppers, anchovies or black olives. But I think we've insulted the bagel enough.

Pizza bagels

Makes 4

olive oil
2 cloves of garlic, crushed or minced
¼–½ teaspoon chilli flakes
1 x 400g tin of tomatoes
¾ teaspoon dried oregano
salt, pepper and sugar
2 bagels, halved
4 slices or about 90g mozzarella (the low-moisture stuff
    that comes pre-sliced)
20g pecorino, grated

1. Heat 2 tablespoons of olive oil in a wide frying pan and when it's hot, cook the garlic and chilli flakes for a minute or two.

2. Add the chopped tomatoes and oregano to the pan. Stir well and crush the tomatoes with the back of your spoon.

3. Season with salt and pepper, and add the sugar a pinch at a time if it's tasting a bit harsh.

4. Cook for about 12–14 minutes on a low heat until it's super-saucy.

5. Meanwhile, drizzle the bagel halves with olive oil and put them under a hot grill until they're lightly golden.

6. Lay one mozzarella slice across each bagel half.

7. Spoon the tomato sauce over the mozzarella.

8. Sprinkle the grated pecorino on top.

9. Grill until bubbly, brown and looking suspiciously like pizza.

Put a cherry on it

Page 35 and time to ask ourselves: what the hell is Laura Goodman talking about? What is she offering us? What kind of book is this?

The maraschino cherry is a very good symbol for me as the author of this book because I do not really like the way they taste (I would donate mine to a dining companion), but I love what they stand for. Am I going to dedicate a whole section of my book to a food whose flavour I don't enjoy but whose essence speaks to me? I think I am. Have I convinced someone to publish an entire book of essences, moods, feelings and light bites? I think I have! Reach for the stars.

The maraschino cherry is a marvel because it implies a perfection or ideal where there would previously only have been wild squirty cream abandon. You can make whatever unseasonal, incoherent sundae you like as long as you finish with one of these shiny, syrupy Rudolph noses.

I adore an unseasonal, incoherent sundae topped with a cherry, and I think it must be an interesting time to be one, because ice cream fans have access to supermarket aisles full of salted caramel pecan pie ooey-gooey brownie doo-wop fandangos, which are essentially consolidated sundaes.

But I do believe there is a specific type of joy to be found in a multi-faceted ice cream snack, thoughtfully assembled by hand, that cannot be found in the frosty bottom of a cardboard tub. So, let's take the ice cream right back to vanilla and dress it up how I (not Ben nor Jerry) see fit.

This is a relatively classic banana split, aside from the peanut buttery hot fudge sauce that smothers it. While the overall aesthetic is quite fifties, you don't really see a banana without a nut butter in the 2020s – it's just not done. And we have no truck with sweet things that aren't at least a little bit salty. Make this beautiful thing for your friend on Friday night – put a maraschino cherry on another wild squirty cream week. That's what I'm offering you.

Hot fudge peanut butter banana split

Makes 4

4 bananas
8 scoops of vanilla ice cream
½ batch of hot fudge PB sauce (as below)
140ml double cream, whipped (or Oatly whippable creamy oat) (or squirty cream)
30g salted roasted peanuts, roughly chopped
sprinkles
4 maraschino cherries

Hot fudge PB sauce

200ml double cream (or Oatly creamy oat)
1½ tablespoons golden syrup

1 tablespoon cocoa powder, sifted
3 tablespoons smooth peanut butter
¼ teaspoon fine sea salt
70g chopped dark chocolate

1. To make the sauce, combine the cream, golden syrup, sifted cocoa powder, peanut butter and salt in a small saucepan over a medium heat and bring it to a low simmer.

2. Whisk for 3–5 minutes – just until everything has melted. Turn the heat off.

3. Add the chocolate pieces to the pan but don't stir them through yet. Tuck them under the cream and wait for one minute, then whisk it through, until you have a sauce that's dark, smooth and glossy.

4. You can transfer this to a jar and (once cooled) keep it in the fridge if you're not using it immediately. It'll firm up, so when you come to use it, you might need to loosen it by running the jar under a warm tap. When it's spoonable, warm up what you need very gently.

5. To assemble a sundae, split a banana lengthways, lay the halves on a plate and lodge 2 scoops of ice cream between them.

6. Spoon warmed-up hot fudge sauce over the ice cream, followed by whipped cream, chopped nuts, sprinkles and a cherry.

SNACKETTES

- A chunk of mozzarella with an anchovy pressed up close.

- An egg-cup of peanut butter.

- A peeled boiled egg with mustard mayo.

- A plain Digestive with cream cheese and jam (fruit cheesecake) or cream cheese and Nutella (chocolate cheesecake).

- Lumps of Parmesan dipped in balsamic.

- Frazzles and Skips in stacks (instant surf and turf).

- A Medjool date stuffed with Gorgonzola.

- Salt and vinegar crisps with taramasalata (instant fish and chips).

- An apple and a cup of tea.

LIFE SNACKS II (Europe)

- A metre of chocolate brioche under an umbrella with a shot of bad espresso somewhere in the 20th arrondissement of Paris. I was alone, so I'd had to use my own voice to order, and I hadn't died of shame or accent or any related cause. I don't know the true length of the brioche but I know that I felt like I'd be eating it forever (and that was fine).

- Pizza con patate from Forno Campo de' Fiori in Rome, rosemary wafting to say *buongiorno* while the pizza was cut into oblongs with scissors. I ate it while perching on the back of someone's trailer.

- A bowl of voluptuous Greek yoghurt – with honey, but free from other modcons – in Folegandros, Greece, the smooth white yoghurt reflecting the sun back at my SPF-smothered face.

- I believe I actually ran to get pastéis de nata in time for a train from Lisbon to Sintra. Looks like it was worth it because here they are! Custardy bastards.

- A slice of red pepper tortilla eaten from the top of a barrel in Rioja with a cold, peachy glass of rosado.

- At a not-ordinary services in northern France, I grabbed a prune pound cake for the road. Then, I gnawed it.

- A basket of calamari with a carafe of local white wine in Dubrovnik. I couldn't say whether this was particularly good squid, but it was a formative holiday snacking experience which opened the floodgates. You never forget your first.

- An almond granita in a sweltering square in Siracusa, with a book. The colour of almond granita – iridescent white, with a whisper of coral where the sun hits it – is what I'd use to paint heaven (if asked).

- Freshly engaged in Málaga, a jug of sangria and the eighth or ninth plate of croquetas.

- I do not understand the performance of the galette man at the Marché des Enfants Rouges in Paris. His queue is long enough to completely kill your vibe and while you're waiting in it, he will periodically make very intense eye contact with you while mouthing the words 'miam miam'. Nonetheless, his 'garnie' galettes are *epique* – the smell of caramelising Emmental and onion engulfs the market, making you powerless to avoid the slightly off-key experience. You'll understand why my friend Janet and I are still laughing, six years later, about the time – after all that waiting – that Rich ordered the 'fraicheur' (salad, tomatoes, parsley).

- I would usually be suspicious of a finger of food as gorgeous as the raspberry and passionfruit eclair from L'Éclair de Génie, so it's lucky that someone who knows their choux gave it to me and changed my life.

- A ball of very fresh mozzarella from a grocery store barrel in Monti in Rome.

- A punnet of tiny gariguette strawberries that tasted like Tootsie Rolls.

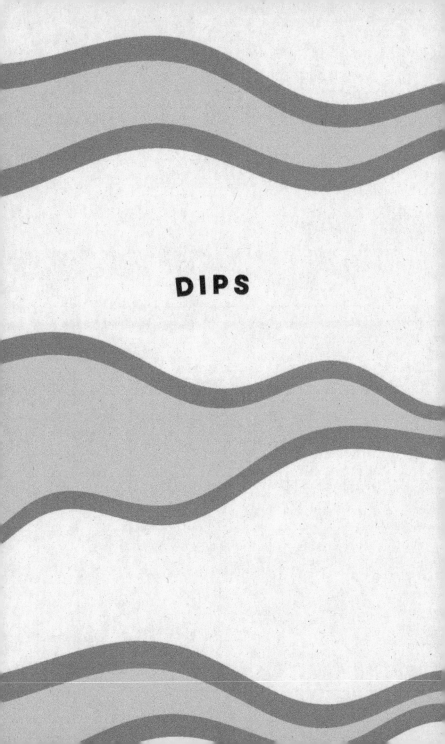

DIPS

Taking a dip

The food arrives. I shift my schmatte out of the frame and wipe my camera lens with my dress; one snap here. Move to the right to escape my own shadow, lean back so my reflection vacates the spoon; another there. Half-heartedly turn the saturation up, and after one bite, two bites, consider a caption, stopping to mmm and raise my eyebrows.

At Mama's Pita on the Cycladic island of Folegandros I wrote: 'Time for a quick dip', with Greek flag and blue heart emojis. Just arrived: one tzatziki, one melitzanosalata, plenty of Mama's bouncy pitta and cold fizzy water. We were hot, salty and pleased with ourselves, pleased in particular with our decision to order dips for lunch. We were constrained only by our own ideas about how the rest of the day might unfold (we want to eat a bigger meal quite soon/let's not spend all our money at once/I don't know if I fancy the full souvla). And OK, I'm no Simone de Beauv, but I tapped out that caption and I thought: mmm. A dip in the sea, dips for lunch; honestly, what could be nicer? How did I get to be a person with free and ready access to precede dips with dips?

At the time, I chose to take a photo instead of 'being in the moment', which is another thing we're sure we don't do enough of, like drinking water, breathing into our bellies and massaging our birth scars. Here I am, trying to bring up a toddler in 2022, doing the best I can in diabolical circumstances, and I'm worried I'm not doing enough of anything or something or nothing at the same time. Over the last few years I have stopped to appreciate so many moments, while simultaneously kicking myself for not appreciating them enough. *This is good, this is so good, I know how good this is. (What a shame my knowing it can never be enough.)* I remember thinking this about hundreds of LA sunsets, hundreds of cups of coffee, hundreds of minutes peering through the slats in my daughter's cot while she giggled about the fact of being awake.

Instead of writing my not-clever caption I suppose I could have discussed the arrival of the dips in more detail with my husband. But why? I was hungry to have that moment more properly, at maximum saturation, just as much of the moment as I possibly could. That's actually what a photo is, not a symbol of your deep-rooted disconnection with Real Things.

If a dip in the sea is living with abandon then the dips in this chapter are the food equivalent. For some of us, the food comes easier. I'm not a natural in the water, so a swim in the sea for me is fraught (you can't see it on Instagram but I'm fighting with my own shoulders, trying to let go of complicated things knotted into my muscles). The same cannot be said of my relationship with tzatziki.

Tzatziki and friends

I have written before about how much I love yoghurt but I'm not actually anyone, so you probably don't know that.

Hello there! I love yoghurt. What I admire most about yoghurt is its ability to flex sweet or savoury, depending on what you have in store for it. It's obliging, which is a rare thing to be these days. I could easily have filled a chapter with tangy, garlicky, lemony dips, but I edited myself down to this terrific little fermented milk trifecta.

Serves 2–3

The base

250g Greek yoghurt (you can use vegan yoghurt, but I would try to get one that's 'Greek-style' and avoid coconut-based)
1 small clove of garlic
2 teaspoons lemon juice
1 tablespoon extra virgin olive oil
flaky sea salt and black pepper (to taste)

1. Spoon the yoghurt into a small bowl.

2. Mince or crush the garlic straight in (I use a Microplane).

3. Add the lemon juice and oil, and stir well.

4. Season, and then . . .

Tzatziki

Grate ½ a cucumber and mix it in a sieve with ½ teaspoon of fine sea salt. Leave the sieve standing over a mixing bowl for

45 minutes, stirring it occasionally. Give it a big squeeze at the end of its hanging time, then stir it into the yoghurt mix.

Lemon and dill
Stir through 2 tablespoons of finely chopped dill and more lemon juice, to taste.

Sizzled chilli butter and pistachio
Melt 40g of salted butter gently in a small pan until it starts to smell hazelnutty. Add ¾ teaspoon of Aleppo chilli flakes and 30g of chopped pistachios and swirl everything round the pan for a minute, watching it foam up. Pour this foamy, nutty butter over the yoghurt and use a spoon to swirl it, just a little.

Heartburn

In Lyon, France, I achieved the worst heartburn of my life. I spent the midnight hours propped into a right angle, waiting for all the pork products I'd consumed to burn my greedy heart out, while my mind spun in its signature dead-of-night style.

I was writing a city guide (we called them Instant Escapes) for my beloved *Sunday Times Travel Magazine* (RIP). These were weird halcyon days; we were all clinging on to a time in which you could actually travel for a living, even though the per word rate had not risen for at least 15 years. Still, I wept at my luck in absurd locations: a balcony in Jamaica's Blue Mountains where fireflies lit up my dinner, a savagely beautiful hotel on the edge of Marrakech's medina and in the giant windows of NYC suites I had no business peering out of.

I was lucky to do this work but by the end, the PRs were pushing for ever more complex mentions 'in return' for my hire car. And actually, had I been weeping at my luck or at my guilt after all? I don't know, but I had to do five other jobs to make life viable. That's what I meant about clinging on.

Anyway, in Lyon, I'd been living it up in the style of an old-fashioned travel journalist at the bouchons, so my heart was burning not just with the guilt, but in a very literal sense. These officially certified Lyonnaise taverns are the burgundy, convivial, ruddy-cheeked restaurants of your dreams, where exclusively obscene food is served (pork crackling with your aperitif, pink praline on your pudding). True bouchons feature the symbol of Gnafron, a wine-loving puppet with a bulbous red nose.

Very occasional relief is provided by cervelle de canut – a herby, tart, fromage blanc-based concoction that's kind of a dip and kind of a spread. The name translates as 'silk-weaver's brain' in a snooty, nuanced and confusing slur on the canuts who wove silk in 19th-century Lyon (their brains are yoghurty? Their brains are good for dipping things in? Their brains require three fresh herbs to work properly?). Anyway, the reality of the dish is decidedly un-brainlike.

Fromage blanc is hard to get outside of France, so I use plain skyr or thick Greek yoghurt. Serve yours in a bowl next to a pile of oil-drizzled toasts, raw vegetables and a bottle of the jolliest-looking Beaujolais you can lay your hands on. This could be the snack to soothe your burning heart.

Cervelle de canut

Serves 4-ish

225g skyr or thick Greek yoghurt
75g crème fraîche
1 clove of garlic, crushed or minced
½ shallot, very finely chopped
1 tablespoon finely chopped tarragon
1 tablespoon finely chopped chives
1 tablespoon finely chopped parsley
1 tablespoon red wine vinegar
extra virgin olive oil
flaky sea salt
black pepper

1. Combine everything but the salt and pepper in a bowl with a tablespoon of olive oil.

2. Season to taste and drizzle the top with more oil.

California wafting

I spent a winter in LA, marching up and down canyons in my leggings, marvelling at technicolour sunsets, pooling Ubers, watching the Atlantic froth to and fro, enjoying the repercussions of cheesy crackers with weed in them, drinking drip coffee and doing HIIT classes at Sweat Garage. And another way of looking at it: I spent three months wafting from one salsa to another. It was salsa that punctuated these perfect days.

At the weekend we'd skulk about the farmers' market slurping our juices like A-listers caught 'loading up on groceries in relaxed sweats', picking up pickled daikon at Dave's Gourmet Korean Food, a tote bag's worth of navel oranges, plus tomatoes and great bushes of cilantro. And then in the week, whenever we sensed a delicious, low-key day drifting to its natural close, we'd start chopping. We'd eat our salsa with handfuls of corn chips from a metre-long bag that never lasted as long as we thought it would. Corn chip by corn chip, this is how we meditated.

Compare and contrast the day on which I wrote the first of these two salsa recipes. At 5 p.m., one December day, when it had been dismally dark for well over an hour, my five-month-old daughter noticed how rapidly her brain had been developing and began to shriek. Meanwhile, it came to my dog's attention that she'd only had the chance to chase six squirrels that day, nowhere near her daily quota. My tiny world softly imploded as I drifted around the house, treading in pools of regurgitated breast milk, counting down the minutes to dinner, which wouldn't actually provide any relief, but would just be something different to do.

I'm never sure if recreating foods you ate in paradise is a good idea. However many limes you squeeze, you're still where you are. It's December, things feel rough and you can't slide the fuzzy filter of hindsight over an evening you're about to have. But sometimes it just takes one sip of lemonade to feel human again, even and especially when you don't believe it's possible. The right straw, the right stroll; out of nowhere, a little service bell chimes in your head and you are briefly awake. So you have to keep seeking slivers of paradise – you just do.

The first of my two salsas is designed to invoke easy, breezy Cali bliss even when you're living soggily and gloomily in a breast-milk puddle. And the second – well, it's for mango season.

Tinned tomatillo salsa

A tomatillo is a little green tomato with a papery husk (same); it's both fruitier and sourer than a tomato and in Mexican cuisine it's used to make The Other Salsa: salsa verde. Tomatillos are not as easy to come by in the UK, which is why I'm delighted to reveal that you can use tinned ones. I've worked hard on this because I think we all need it: a zangy dip capable of picking us up from winter's floor. This salsa is good without the avocado, but all the creamier, greener and more day-making for it. Get through this pot of green stuff as meditatively as you possibly can, while you calmly google 'last-minute holidays'.

Serves 4-ish

1 x 11oz (300-ish-gram) tin of tomatillos
½ brown onion, roughly chopped
20g fresh coriander leaves
2 jalapeños, deseeded and roughly chopped
1 avocado
salt, to taste

1. Drain the tomatillos and arrange them on a foil-covered grill pan. Place them under a hot grill and watch them closely, turning as often as you need to char them all over. Let them cool.

2. Blend the blackened tomatillos with the other ingredients and 100ml of cold water until completely smooth.

3. Thin with a little more cold water if you like, and season to taste.

Mango salsa

Talk about a good-time gal(sa). No word-pairing better signifies sun and fun and goodness in your garden than 'mango salsa'. Oh, OK then, maybe one other: 'Um Bongo'. Fine, a serious one: 'pina colada' (page 206). This salsa is sweet, tart, fresh and just really sunny to look at. Pump up your becobwebbed paddling pool and let's get this fiesta started.

Serves 2-ish

1 red onion, finely chopped
100ml cider vinegar
2 mangoes (ideally almost-but-not-quite-ripe; if they're too ripe, yours will be a smushy sort-of salsa, which isn't necessarily a bad thing, provided you're ready for it)
15g fresh coriander leaves, roughly chopped
1 tablespoon finely chopped fresh mint
1 red pepper

2 jalapeños

juice of 3 limes (-ish! But have extra on standby, always)

sea salt

1. To quickly and lightly pickle the finely chopped onion, put it into a sieve and pour a kettle-full of boiling water over it. Then put it into a small bowl with the cider vinegar. It'll be rosy in 30 minutes.

2. Free as much mango from the stones as possible, then finely chop and tip into whatever bowl you're using to contain the salsa.

3. Add the chopped herbs to the bowl.

4. Deseed and finely chop the pepper and jalapeños and add those to the bowl, too.

5. Lift out the onion pieces from the vinegar and add those to the salsa bowl – it's OK to take a bit of residual vinegar with you.

6. Squeeze over the lime juice and toss everything gently with a fork.

7. Season with salt to taste.

Serves four, generously

When did we start defaulting to hummus? Now there's an unlikely star. Or, not a star exactly, but a member of the ensemble cast of everyday life. A familiar face, like Ian Beale's – you'd miss him if he went off to live in an underpass for a bit, but otherwise you hardly notice he's there. At some point, we started to eat so much hummus that now the supermarket sells red pepper, beetroot, sweet chilli, caramelised onion, piri piri, turmeric and smoked hummuses. Maybe most bamboozlingly of all, as sure a sign of a decrepit society as any, it sells reduced fat hummus. Consider please that we took the time to reduce the fat contained in a product made of chickpeas, tahini, lemon and (if you're lucky) olive oil. We have absolutely no idea what we're doing.

We carry hummus with us. We take it to picnics, yes, but also to work and to people's houses when we're not sure what the lunch situation is going to be and we don't want to be overbearing. It hits the spot, everyone likes it and you're never going to find a Tesco Express that doesn't sell it. The cynics would say it's a symbol of our busy lifestyles – that we no longer have the time to make ourselves real food. They'd have to concede that it's 'better' than drinking White Lightning.

On *Celebrity Gogglebox*, Nick Grimshaw scorned 'people who make hummus, when it costs 45p to buy' and it got me where it hurts (which *Gogglebox*, the nation's comfort blanket, is not meant to do) because he is right and yet, look at me, I do make hummus. And I make it with jarred chickpeas which cost so much money. If you were doing an affordability check on me, looking closely at my ingoings and outgoings to determine whether or not I deserved to borrow money from you at an exorbitant rate, what I guarantee you would find is that the brand of chickpeas I buy does not correlate with my income. But I do buy them, and

I do make hummus with them. I reserve the chickpea liquor to add back in gradually at the end until the hummus is light and moussey like Georgina Hayden advised me to do on Instagram and in her wonderful book, *Taverna*. The hummus you buy at the supermarket is fine, I don't have a problem with it, but you wouldn't say it's moussey, would you? I sound absurd, I know, but you have to live your truth, and mine is a mousse.

Supermarket hummus, as well as coming in very many flavours, takes multiple formats, one of which is the mini snack pot. The idea, as I understand it, is that you throw the mini snack pot into your tote bag alongside a novel you can't get into – a bag of whatevers thrown together seconds before you slam the front door and walk smack into a day you're not ready for. And the opposite of a mini snack pot of hummus isn't hummus made expensively with chickpeas from a jar, because that's just something you do when your life has taken a certain ridiculous, delicatessenish turn. I think in fact the opposite of a mini snack pot of hummus is a big hot bubbling tray of cheese, sour cream and mayo-based dip, the kind you see Americans talking about around the time of the Super Bowl.

These are dips as centrepieces not as afterthoughts. They are super bowls. A dip like this is a huge palaver to carry around, but you do it because the palaver is worthwhile (which I guess was Nick Grimshaw's quite reasonable point – how could making something you can get so easily be worthwhile?).

These are warm, cheesy, slow and thoughtful dips that scream generosity, and they're not just for you, but for three or four of your best people. You might eat one while you have a very comprehensive chat, using it as a big, warm anchor at the heart of the table while you get to the nub of the matter, as you always do. You don't actually need anything on your agenda apart from this dip. You could watch sport if you wanted to, or a *Married at First Sight* reunion or *My Big Fat Greek Wedding* for the 700th time, but you could also just sit around eating this dip and that's it, that's the night.

At our friends' daughter's second birthday party, my friend Clare brought a tray of hot spinach dip and two bags of crostini to eat with it. It wasn't the kind of party where you were expected to bring things and I thought it was so nice that she had brought it, even while we struggled with the oven and she became increasingly self-conscious. (And so you know, I'm reasonably kind, too: I brought a banana bread, but I just slammed it lovelessly on the kitchen worktop without saying a word.) What Clare had made (and carried across London) was a heaping cosy tray to share, the sort of food that emanates joy.

Since then, I've spent a bit of time sitting with these dips, thinking about what makes them great. I have two clear favourites. One is oniony because nothing says *I love you, my friends* like sweet, golden onions. And the other is crabby, because crab and Gruyère is one of the most celebratory combos in the world.

Hot roasted onion dip

Serves 4–6

375g mixed red and brown onions, sliced
35ml olive oil, plus a little extra
1½ teaspoons picked thyme leaves
sea salt
1 head of garlic
280g cream cheese
180g sour cream
75g mozzarella, torn to shreds
65g Gruyère, grated
black pepper
plenty of crostini, to serve

1. Preheat the oven to 180°C/160°C fan/gas 4.

2. Pile the sliced onions into a small oven dish. Toss with the oil, thyme and two big pinches of sea salt.

3. Lop the top from the head of garlic so the cloves are exposed. Rub the exposed ends with a drizzle more oil, then make a gap in your onion-scape and slot the bulb in snugly, cut side down.

4. Roast for 50–55 minutes, tossing the onions halfway through. By the end, some onions will be crispy and charred but most will be sticky.

5. Squeeze the roasted garlic out of the bulb on to a chopping board and mash it with a fork. Next to it, finely chop the roasted onions.

6. In a large saucepan set over a low heat, combine the cream cheese and sour cream and stir until even. Add the mozzarella, Gruyère and several twists of black pepper and keep stirring until everything's melted into a stretchy, creamy dream.

7. Stir through the garlic and onions.

8. Check for seasoning before you tip the dip into a bowl and go in with your crostini.

Hot crab and Gruyère dip

Serves 4–6

180g cream cheese
180g sour cream
50g mayonnaise
½ teaspoon smoked paprika
¼ teaspoon ground nutmeg
½ teaspoon finely grated lemon zest
2 teaspoons lemon juice
1 tablespoon Worcestershire sauce
100g mixed crabmeat
60g Gruyère (and an extra 20g for the top)
15g Parmesan
salt and pepper

2 spring onions, chopped and split into green and white
   bits
cucumber, carrots and crackers to serve (I like a big red
   box of Ritz)

1. Preheat the oven to 180°C/160°C fan/gas 4.

2. You can mix this in the small oven dish you're going to
    bake it in. Beat the cream cheese, sour cream and may-
    onnaise together until smooth and even.

3. Add everything else except the extra 20g of Gruyère
    and the green bits of the spring onions, and mix until
    evenly combined. Season with salt and pepper to taste.

4. Sprinkle the extra 20g of Gruyère on top and bake for
    25 minutes, until the top is bubbly and brown.

5. Leave to cool for a few minutes before sprinkling on the
    greens of the spring onion and dipping in.

It's a small world, after all

Everywhere I've ever been tastes of something, and it might
be the thing you expect, or it might not be. Enjoy your ride
through my brain! Please keep your hats, glasses and water
bottles inside the carriage at all times.

Copenhagen is smoked fish.
London is a Pret tuna baguette.
Paris is a slice of terrine.
LA is a breakfast taco.
Melbourne is a flat white.

Barcelona is a razor clam.

Lisbon is custard.

New York City is an iced coffee.

Mexico City is sponge cake with sprinkles.

Bangkok is a polystyrene container of mango sticky rice.

North-west London is a smoked salmon bagel.

Auckland is a chunky dip.

Cashew, kale and Parmesan dip

This dip sits somewhere between a chopped kale salad and a pesto – too blitzed to be eaten with a fork, too full of crunchy cashews to envelop your gnocchi. It scoops like a dream, as long as you have the correct tools (crisps or pitta chips).

Texture is everything here (Auckland is a *chunky* dip, I said), so if you have an over-zealous food processor (or you're using a bullet-style blender), you need to be gentle, pulsing the ingredients as tentatively as you can. If you don't trust yourself, chop or crush the cashews by hand. I have eaten this amount of dip by myself but as we have established, I am dip mad. If you want to make more you can double the recipe but (not to harp on) you'll definitely need to pulse in batches.

Serves 2-ish

70g cashews
50g kale

10g fresh basil leaves
1 small clove of garlic
juice of ½ lemon
140ml extra virgin olive oil
25g chunk of Parmesan (you could leave this out or use a
   dairy-free wedge)
salt and pepper

1. Pulse the cashews tentatively in a food processor or grind them in a pestle and mortar. You're looking for coarse chunks, not sand. Tip them into a bowl or Tupperware.

2. Back in the food processor, pulse the kale (stalks and all), basil leaves, garlic, lemon juice and half the olive oil until the ingredients are combined in a chunky green mulch. Scrape this into the bowl with the cashews.

3. Grate the Parmesan straight into the bowl.

4. Add the rest of the olive oil and stir well with a fork.

5. Season with salt and pepper to taste.

LIFE SNACKS III (London)

- I'll never forget the first time Rich brought home beef empanadas from Pueblito Paisa in Seven Sisters. I'll never forgive how he casually revealed he'd been eating them regularly for months.

- The neighbourhood restaurant of everyone's dreams existed in Hackney in another time and it was called Railroad. I spent a lot of time there with people I don't know any more, eating freeform crumpets sopping with melted butter and honey.

- Fortnum & Mason Chocolossus biscuits at Christmas. It was the height of the gold tin; it was the majestic palm tree on the front; it was the thickness of the chocolate. Who am I kidding? It was the word chocolossus.

- Naan breads from Ararat Bread on Ridley Road, torn from the bag at the cinema.

- Popcorn chicken with plum, chilli, seaweed or curry seasoning shaken all over it from Good Friend on Little Newport Street, specifically the time we took my 18-month-ish daughter to show her what London looked like in an easing of lockdowns. 'Crispy!' she said.

- One scoop of ricotta and sour cherry gelato from Gelupo.

- The first time I ate one of Calum Franklin's pork pies, I happened to have a manicure to befit its beauty. The whole scene looked like something from the Palace of Versailles, in my opinion.

- Callaloo patties from Rainbow Bakery in Dalston, after a fringe trim.

- A spinach and feta gözleme with a Diet Coke.

- A lahmacun wrap filled with salad, pickles, garlic sauce and chilli sauce on a long walk home from a work trip to a dusty one-day music festival, by my beloved self. Nothing tastes better than leaving a work party.

CARBY THINGS

Here she goes again, I know, but I'm no pretender, and what is your careful little snack plate without a hunk of bread? What curbs an urge and swiftly warms a belly like stodge? What good is your onion dip, or your nacho sauce or your country-style terrine without a potato to lie on or a cracker to be scooped with? This is a little chapter to say: we really do love carbs, don't we? I wasn't making it up. You'll find all the bready things and latkes you need right here. And – why not? Lean in and all that – fried spaghetti.

Things on toast

I was given a book called *Things on Toast* when I was 24, still discovering that vegetarian food could be nice and fruit-cake could be eaten with cheese. I can't find it now so I think I must've passed it on when I believed I'd made some kind of culinary ascension, and would now only be troubling myself with cookbooks that were considered canon. After that, as I grew a little self-aware and a lot jaded, I came to understand that certain cookbooks are considered good and proper as a direct result of systems built to steal the limelight from writers who aren't white or posh and don't bang on about the importance of 'good, simple ingredients' enough (especially, I think, boiled ham?). The canon can go swivel.

Things on Toast might not have been important to Them but it was important to me because I'd never have thought, at that time, to group food in that way and make a book out of it. I had never paused to think about the versatility of toast, which is interesting considering that's all I do now. That and more harried rumination on the point of it all, and whether I'm living well, and about my age and whether I'm doing enough Pilates, and how I don't feel like I've learned anything since I was at university (studying English, because I thought it was more worthwhile than American Studies or Dance). But look at it this way: in 2009, I found the book *Things on Toast* to be revelatory. Imagine what I'd have made of a book about snacks. I guess it really is a journey. And every day (if you're lucky), there's toast.

Here are two toasts you might not have thought about yet.

'Nduja, mascarpone and honey toast

In London in 2009, there were no pizzas beyond the chains. Overnight, the words 'dough balls', 'Hawaiian' and 'stuffed crust' met their matches with the buzzier 'sourdough', 'Neapolitan' and 'fior de latte'. Corners of neighbourhoods sprouted brown paper menus, unbreakable glass tumblers, bottles of chilli oil, rockety side salads and wirework bar stools. We got pizza merch, pizza collabs and brunch pizzas topped with far-flung sausages. I now live in a London neighbourhood in which you could eat a pizza from a different joint every night of the week – and other than that, there is nothing restauranty to speak of. In this unexpected life of surplus pizza, Sodo's Wicker Man slams them all. Its toppings are a ferocious puddle of creamy mascarpone and spicy 'nduja, with honey trickling deliciously across the top.

Come on! It's a riot. And although I try to be very careful not to overdo the Wicker Man, I have developed this little toast to keep me going. It's just a grilled combination of things that in the end tastes – well – restauranty.

I've given rough amounts for 4 toasts to help you shop, but after that, please be free (to do what you want to do, you've got to live your life (do what you want to do)).

80g 'nduja
4 slices of any rustic bread
120g mascarpone
honey
flaky sea salt

1. Thickly spread the 'nduja straight on to the sliced bread.

2. Drop generous spoonfuls of mascarpone on top and, using a knife, smush it into the 'nduja, mixing the two together just a little.

3. Place the bread under a hot grill, until the toppings are oozy.

4. Drizzle on plenty of honey (when you think you've got enough, add more) and sprinkle with flaky salt.

Roasted garlic toast

You're either looking for uncomplicated ways to consume roasted garlic, freshly squeezed from the bulb, or you're not. My husband skews towards horrified and I skew towards thank goodness you don't want any, I'll eat the whole thing in one sitting, hold the bread. This recipe is a reminder that you don't really need an occasion to roast two bulbs of garlic. It doesn't need to be Christmas and you don't need a whole hot Camembert to go with it. The 'spreadable goat's cheese' in the ingredients list refers to those supermarket tubs that are almost pyramids – do you know the ones? But as you have probably gathered, I'd happily eat this toast without any cheese at all. Or toast.

Rough amounts for 4 toasts

2 whole bulbs of garlic
olive oil
4 slices of any rustic bread
100g spreadable goat's cheese (optional)
honey
flaky sea salt

1. Preheat the oven to 140°C/120°C fan/gas 1.

2. With each bulb of garlic, slice the very tops off, keeping the bulbs intact, so that the cloves are all (or mostly all) exposed.

3. Splash a puddle of olive oil into a small oven dish and season with salt and pepper. Place the bulbs cut side down and rub them in the oil a little.

4. Leave the bulbs cut side down and cover the dish with a baking tray. Roast in the oven for 1 hour.

5. Toast the bread and drizzle with olive oil.

6. Spread each slice with goat's cheese (if you're using it), then squeeze the cloves of garlic directly from their papery wrappers on top of the cheese.

7. Drizzle with honey and sprinkle with flaky salt.

SNACKETTES, QUICK TOAST EDITION

- Olive oil, sliced cucumber, salt.

- Olive oil, chunks of feta, olives, tomatoes.

- Ricotta and cherry jam.

- Tahini, honey, flaky salt.

- Cream cheese, cinnamon sugar (brûléed a touch under the grill).

- Olive oil, melted dark chocolate (lots), almond butter, flaky salt.

- Butter and honey (to melt), slices of Gruyère or Comté (cold).

Crumpet season

Welcome to September. The tree directly outside our house doesn't do much, but some of the trees round the corner look like actual, fantastical phoenixes on fire, and I'm compelled to pick up fallen leaves, adore them all the way home and then do nothing with them. I'm wearing a bit of burgundy or forest green and I've got a fluffy coat on, though I don't yet cling to it for dear life; it's not freezing. Maybe I am finally evolving into a real person because I used to believe cold was just cold. When the sky is blue now, I'm shocked, and I repeat that the sky is blue over and over again until it's gone, obscured in totality by the grey clouds which are apparently the same clouds they get all over the world, but which seem uniquely, dankly British.

Anyway, I've just remembered: autumn isn't good. Or, if it's a bit good, it doesn't last for very long. The leaves are pretty and the pubs are cosy but I now have to buckle my boots for eight straight months, take dog walks in the bog, layer myself up to get some eggs from Tesco. I'll be a soggy, mangled, inside-out umbrella person, dashing to the bus stop in the dark. It's here, the longest season of the year, or as I like to think of it, for my sanity: crumpet season.

Nothing comforts like a crumpet. Often, things categorised as 'comfort food' are just food: food that isn't salad, food that's hot and maybe has cheese on it. But by any definition, a bouncy, buttery crumpet requires almost no effort and will soothe whatever ails you, even if all that ails you is the fact another grey day has arrived.

Once you've been outside, a crumpet can also be a helpful tool for remembering why you love your home, if you are lucky enough to have a lovable home. Maybe earlier today you were obsessing over scuff marks up a wall, or a chipped kitchen counter, or a blotchy, dog-stained carpet. But now, look. Here is a crumpet and a cup of tea. Didn't you *just* take a teabag from the beautiful caddy your goddaughter sent you for your birthday? Can you imagine your kitchen without that big, weird porcelain egg you bought at a flea market? Didn't you choose the blue on the walls to remind you of the goodness of the sky? It's OK.

Three crumpets

You're probably perfectly secure in the crumpet toppings you've spent your life honing. I understand. My go-to duo is: one Marmite, one honey and salt. But as I mentioned, the season is long and arduous. To get through it, you've got no choice but to use your crumpet. Here are three ways to do so.

Cheddar cheese and lime pickle

Of course any beloved pickle or chutney will serve you well, but there's something special about this sharp and fiery combo. I like sliced cold Cheddar on a hot buttered crumpet with a dollop of lime pickle on top. But you could also melt the cheese under the grill.

Apricot jam and goat's cheese

Butter and jam your crumpet, and crumble some goat's cheese on top.

Date and treacle

In a blender or food processor, blitz 75g of softened salted butter (or vegan block butter) with 50g of pitted dates and ½ teaspoon of black treacle. Mazel tov, you've got sticky toffee crumpets for the week.

Latkes

My dad's family is Jewish and my mum's is Catholic and my Chrismukkah is as slipshod as the next guy's (I'm trying, there's a lot going on). We've got a menorah and some opinion-dividing tinsel and a Christmas tree with a polar bear on the top. Two of my favourite December things are: crispy potato latkes served with sour cream and apple sauce, and trees spangled with lights and lametta. Put them together and what have you got? Bibbidi bobbidi bauble: frying latkes as you decorate the tree. This is a composite tradition I invented – did you know you can just make them up? In fact, now that you're an adult, it's incumbent on you to do so. Choose to syrup your spaghetti like Buddy the Elf or choose to fill a musical biscuit tin with seasonal Nespresso capsules or choose to eat snacks for dinner in the luminous glow of your fairy lights. Here are my golden latkes, glistening like the snow in the lane (but with fat).

Makes 12–14

900g potatoes (Maris Pipers or King Edwards, ideally)
2 large onions
2 eggs

3½ tablespoons matzo meal
2 teaspoons fine sea salt
black pepper
goose or chicken fat (optional)
rapeseed oil
flaky sea salt
apple sauce and sour cream to serve

1. Peel the potatoes and onions and grate them through the large holes of a box grater into one big starchy mass.

2. Tip this mass into the middle of a clean tea towel and wring it out over the sink, losing as much moisture as you possibly can. Crispy latkes are won or lost here.

3. In a large bowl, combine the eggs, matzo meal, salt and several twists of black pepper and mix it all together using a fork.

4. Add the potato and onion to the bowl and mix with your hands until everything's evenly coated with egg.

5. Heat your oven to 140°C/120°C fan/gas 1, and – near the hob – have a few sheets of kitchen paper ready on a plate.

6. To begin frying, add 6 tablespoons of fat to a medium frying pan (either a mix of goose or chicken fat and oil for that schmaltzy flavour, or just oil). You want the fat to be almost a centimetre deep at all times, so you'll need to keep topping up.

7. Heat the pan over a medium heat and test the oil temperature with a scrap of latke mix – if the fat sizzles as soon as the potato hits it, you're good to go.

8. Form an oval-shaped piece in your hands (about 2–3 tablespoons of mix, remembering you have enough for 12–14 latkes) and put it straight into the hot fat, flattening it gently with the back of a spatula but keeping it at least a centimetre thick.

9. Fry the latkes in batches until both sides are deep golden brown (about 4 minutes per side). Drain them on the kitchen paper, sprinkle on some flaky salt, and keep the plate warm in the oven.

10. Serve with festive quantities of apple sauce and sour cream.

If you want to quickly make your own apple sauce, just peel, core and roughly chop 3 apples and put them into a small pan over a low heat with the juice of ½ a lemon, 2 teaspoons of sugar and a pinch of salt. Cook them until they're really soft, then either mash them with a spoon or blend them until smooth. Add more sugar to taste.

Snackwiches

My husband Rich is the kind of person who can occasionally become so engrossed in what he's doing that he forgets to eat lunch. So, if he's had a long day out, I will ask what he's eaten, because I'm interested, but also because it gives him a chance to notice if he hasn't eaten anything at all. Rich is also the kind of person who finds the golden arches thoroughly irre-sistible. It's not simply that he enjoys a McDonald's; it's that he finds it difficult to drive past one without stopping for a catch-up with his friend, Big Mac (and three Chicken Selects).

He wouldn't think of this as lunch, though. He'd think of it as a snack. So if I were to ask him if he'd had lunch yet, his most likely response would be: 'No. Oh, well – I had a sand-wich.' That means: not lunch exactly, but I did eat something you might consider to be reasonably substantial, and it was *an item of food consisting of two pieces of bread with a filling between them*, which happens to be the Oxford Languages definition of 'sandwich'.

I investigated this with my team of researchers, two of the leaders in the Snackdonald field: Rich himself, and my friend Janet. We concluded that a Snackdonalds is a pur-chase of one or two products, and anything more than that is a meal. So, a small Snackdonalds would be anything from the 99p menu (fries, a McFlurry or a cheeseburger, for instance), a medium Snackdonalds would be two cheese-burgers (because they really are small) and a large Snackdonalds would be Rich's regular order.

What was interesting to us and probably isn't interesting to you (although hopefully it's a bit interesting because there are some pretty fascinating theories about cheese plates coming up and I wouldn't want you to drop before you reach them) is that a drink counts as an item. To illustrate: if Rich were to add one portion of fries to his regular order, it would become a meal. But if he were to add an Oasis Zero in place of the fries (he would never), that would be a meal, too. We think, but we're not sure, since we invented this whole meaningless theory off the top of our heads via WhatsApp on a Wednesday morning, that it comes down to the number of hands you need to consume your order. You can't throw a McDonald's soda in your bag for later, which means you need to find somewhere to consume your three products, which means – my dear, thank you for sticking with it – you're having a meal.

We can test the theory by visiting the other side of the sandwich spectrum: a stacked deli sandwich on rye (turkey and slaw, or salt beef) from B & K Salt Beef Bar, which I grew up visiting. I would always think of these life-giving, paper-wrapped parcels as meals. Why? Because I wouldn't even consider ordering one without chicken soup and latkes on the side. Oh, and because they're massive. Theory schmeary.

Tuna melt

As far as I'm concerned, a tuna melt is a quicker, easier, oozier (and, yes, fishier) kind of cheeseburger. So let's eat one right now.

An A+ tuna mix calls for generosity with the mayonnaise plus one briny thing (capers or olives) and one onion thing (spring or red). It needs less of the last two things than you think, chopped smaller than you think.

Bread-wise, you need something robust like pain de campagne or sourdough; both of which go gloriously golden when they're slathered with butter and fried.

What's really important is the gherkin you serve on the side. This guy must give your tuna melt the courage to say 'I'm a deli sandwich' and it must act as a bridge between the cheese and the tuna. For a hard-working gherkin, turn to Mrs Elswood Haimisha Cucumbers, which aren't remotely sweet and are chunky enough to sink your teeth into. On this occasion, dainty cornichons need not apply.

Makes 2–3 sandwiches

160g tin of tuna
4 tablespoons mayonnaise
⅛ red onion or the white and pale green parts of a small
    spring onion, finely chopped
1 teaspoon capers or 3–4 olives, finely chopped
salt and black pepper
85g mature Cheddar cheese, sliced
pain de campagne or sourdough, sliced
extra mayonnaise or butter
gherkins, cut lengthways into spears

1. Drain the tuna and mix it with the mayonnaise, onion and olives or capers with a pinch of salt and several twists of black pepper. Taste it and adjust accordingly.

2. You have enough tuna for 2 or 3 sandwiches. To make one, diligently spread the tuna mix with a fork on one slice of bread and arrange the cheese slices to cover. Top with another slice of bread to make a sandwich.

3. Spread the top of the sandwich with butter or mayonnaise.

4. Heat a large frying pan over a medium flame and, when it's hot, put the sandwich in, buttered side down.

5. Use a plate, saucepan lid or any other weight of your choosing to apply downward pressure to the sandwich (I've been known to draw for a pestle and mortar, YOLO).

6. When the underside of the sandwich is golden, butter or mayo the top and flip it. Weigh it down again and fry until both sides are perfectly golden.

7. Serve with gherkins.

No-knead, yes-prod therapy focaccia

Over the course of writing this book, I made a great many focaccias and I didn't even resent it, because putting my fingers through bubbly, slippery dough to make dimples is one of the great black-cloud lifters. What I learned is that focaccia dough is here for me in more ways than just that. It will sit quietly, like my good dog who knows she'll be walked when it stops raining, gently bending and flexing around my day. I've written this recipe slightly differently in an attempt to show you what I mean.

There's no kneading, which means you don't have to clean up any sticky hellscapes. You just mix the ingredients in a bowl and come back to the dough intermittently when you're ready. You return three times in all to 'turn' the dough (more on that below), but the amount of time you're gone for is up to you. Generally the more time you have, the better the flavour, but you'll get a delicious focaccia whatever you do.

Therapy puts a spring in my step and so does this bread.

ACCEPTABLE RISE TIMES

45 minutes to 4 hours *outside the fridge*
8–24 hours *inside the fridge*

HOW TO 'TURN' THE DOUGH

Rich started using the Tartine method for 'basic country bread' that uses turns instead of kneading and from there we became obsessed with not-kneading, because we're always trying our best to get a grip on our kitchen and our lives and having dough everywhere just isn't part of our plan.

To perform a turn, grab the underside of the top of the dough, stretch it up and fold it back over the rest of the dough. Turn the dough 90 degrees and repeat. Do this two more times until you've 'folded' the dough four times. That's one turn.

At the beginning, the turns can feel a little conceptual, and that's fine. As they go on, the dough will get bubblier and busier, but you'll also find you're able to stretch out a flap at the top for a more encompassing fold.

THINGS TO THINK ABOUT IN BETWEEN TURNS

- Can you fall off an infinity pool if you close your eyes on your lilo?

- Why is being too cold worse than being too hot?

- Is butter a snack?

- As my dad once asked, out of nowhere: what happened to Dido?

- How far you've come.

THINGS TO DO IN BETWEEN TURNS

- Walk your pet.

- Touch your toes.

- See a movie.

- Cry.

- Whatever it is you need to do.

THINGS TO TELL YOURSELF IN BETWEEN TURNS, C/O *SEINFELD, PEEP SHOW* AND DR BECKY KENNEDY'S PARENTING INSTAGRAM (@drbeckyat-goodinside)

- Cool wet grass.

- Serenity now.

- My house is a mess, I am not a mess.

- None of this is about me.

- I am a good person, making a focaccia.

THE INGREDIENTS

500g strong white bread flour
5.5g fast-action yeast
15g fine sea salt
400g water (tepid to warm)
at least 130ml extra virgin olive oil
2 red onions
3 big sprigs of rosemary
100g little green olives from a giant jar
flaky sea salt

THE METHOD

1. Mix together the flour, yeast and salt with a fork.

2. Make a well in the middle and add the water. Bring the ingredients together with a spatula and then your hands. When you've finished, the dough will be shaggy and lumpy, but there'll be no floury bits in the bowl.

3. Use a scraper to scrape any dough stuck to the bowl downward to the middle, then drizzle 60ml of extra virgin olive oil around the edges of the dough. Proceed to the first turn.

4. **Turn #1**

5. Cover the bowl with a tea towel before you leave it. If you're going for a shorter rise, leave it in the warmest spot in the house.

6. **Rise #1**

7. **Turn #2**

8. **Rise #2**

9. Flop the dough out of the bowl on to a lipped baking tray – oil, bubbles and all.

10. Do **Turn #3** here in the tray.

11. Leave it here for **Rise #3.**

12. After this final rise, the dough should be soft and billowy, and it should have almost filled the tray. Form claws with your hands and use your fingertips to poke dimples through the dough – you can dig right down to the tray – and while you're doing so, coax the dough closer to the edges of the tray, too.

13. Heat the oven to 240°C/220°C fan/gas 9 and prep your toppings: cut the onions into wedges and pick the leaves from the rosemary sprigs. Drain the olives and leave them whole.

14. Scatter the toppings over the dough, along with 50ml more extra virgin olive oil and some flaky sea salt.

15. Bake the focaccia for 18–20 minutes, or until golden brown all over (but especially at the edges) and bouncy to touch. If it's still very pale in the middle, give it 2 more minutes.

16. As a final act of love, pour extra oil into the dimples.

Spaghetti fritters

Giving us that chapter finale, carpe-diem realness: these freeform fried pasta blobs. They're serving carbs, cheese, crispy bits, creamy dip, whimsicality and insouciance – many of the core tenets of this book. Is it clear to you that I'm having a nice time?

Makes 12-ish

110g spaghetti
finely grated zest of 1 lemon
3 cloves of garlic, crushed or minced
15g parsley, finely chopped
65g Parmesan, finely grated
1–2 teaspoons chilli flakes
1 tablespoon plain flour
1 egg
salt and pepper
20g breadcrumbs
vegetable oil, for frying

For the dip

olive oil
1 small clove of garlic, crushed or minced
150ml double cream
30g Parmesan, finely grated
black pepper
lemon juice

1. Snap your spaghetti in half and cook it. Drain it and rinse it with cold water.

2. Meanwhile, in a bowl, combine the lemon zest, garlic, parsley, Parmesan, chilli flakes, flour, egg, a pinch of salt and a few twists of black pepper.

3. To make the dip, heat a teaspoon or so of olive oil over a low heat and fry the garlic. Stir in the double cream and then the cheese, a pinch of salt and a few twists of black pepper. Stir until the cheese is melted, then turn off the heat and add a big squeeze of lemon.

4. Back to the fritters: add the cooked and cooled spaghetti and the breadcrumbs to the bowl. Toss until everything's evenly dispersed.

5. Heat a couple of centimetres of vegetable oil in a wide frying pan and – near the hob – have a few sheets of kitchen paper ready on a plate.

6. Test the oil temperature with a strand of spaghetti – if the fat sizzles as the pasta hits it, you're good to go.

7. Twirl a fritter's worth of the 'batter' on a fork and lower it into the oil, flattening it a bit with the back of your fork. Repeat a couple of times.

8. Cook the fritters until their undersides are pale golden, then turn over and briefly cook on the other side. I like there to be some crunchy spaghetti and some soft, so pale golden is plenty golden.

9. Rest the fritters on the kitchen paper.

10. Serve them hot, with the Parmesan cream on the side.

STOLEN SNACKS

I

In 1997 I had never heard the word 'baguette' but we some-times got a French stick for a treat from big Tesco. I'm just going to eat the knobbly end, I'd say from the passenger seat, where I'd placed the French stick diagonally across my lap, avoiding the gearstick, which I had no business with. You can't use the knobbly end for a sandwich anyway, can you, Mum. I might as well eat it. I'm just going to tidy it up before we get home. I'm just going to eat half of this French stick, all right, Mum, pretend you can't see.

II

It was a Sunday in 1995 and for reasons I did not yet under-stand, the chicken came out of the oven before everything else. From the garden you could run in and get a bit of skin off a wing or something and it's not that they wouldn't notice, just that they wouldn't bother telling you off. A little bit of crispy gold from under there, so what? But it had that new garlic salt on it, that was the problem. So by the time the potatoes were ready, the chicken wasn't gold any more, but bald. There was no telling-off, but no one got any skin with their dinner, and how did that make me feel?

III

All impatient people know how you snack when dinner isn't ready. You circle the kitchen, peering into pans, stirring things that are better left alone, so that the cook wants to kill you. You ask questions you know to be unbearable:

'Are you going to put any sugar in that?'

'You're going to chop the capers up a bit, aren't you?'

'Why didn't you use the hot paprika?'

Finally, you cut a wedge from the corner of a block of Cheddar. Something to sink your teeth into. (The corner of a block of Cheddar is a snack; a slice is just a slice.)

IV

On any given Friday night at Claudia's house in 2002, some of us had got there in time for dinner and others of us had been out late driving cabs. Some of us were 17 and some of us were 71. Some of us had eaten three courses, driven into the West End pretending to be adults and come back again. Whoever you were, wherever you'd been, there was something you needed to know: the cold roast potatoes were in the fridge.

V

Mum used the tin opener to cut two small slots in the top of the evaporated milk tin so you could pour it on your crumble. The leftovers went into the fridge. And even though sipping through metal didn't feel fantastic, I did it all the time. I opened the fridge, grabbed the tin, and glugged sweet, cold, glossy, beige not-quite-cream straight through the pouring slot. Twenty-five years later, I said: Mum, you know I used to drink the evaporated milk from the tin? You must've known! I drank *so much* of it. Ha, she said, so did I.

CHEESY THINGS

It is impossible to imagine a snacking life without cheese. It sorts out those salty, savoury hankerings every time. Plus, it melts (bubbles and browns, even), occasionally stretches and effortlessly hosts all your favourite condiments. If you start discussing beloved snacks with friends who have moved countries, you usually find that the snacks they love and miss the most are the cheesy ones. And even if you're dairy free, you are likely dousing crispy things in nutritional yeast and craving oozy 'cheesy' queso dips.

Snacks and cheese are inseparable, which is why there is cheese absolutely everywhere in this book – enveloping the potato nachos and the popcorn, lacing the hot dips and the pinwheels, melting on the bagels and the toasts. Honestly, at points it's hard to see the wood for the cheese. Nonetheless, it seemed important to give cheese a chapter of its own – a special place for the heroes, the centrepieces, the balls. But before we get into that, here's a little list to make you think.

Shop-bought cheese-flavoured snacks I have loved

Cheezels
White Cheddar Cheez-Its
Extra Toasty Cheez-Its
Goldfish Crackers

TUC Cheese Sandwiches
Mini Cheddars
Mini Cheddars – Ploughman's Cheshire Cheese
Cheddars (full size)
Wotsits
M&S Cheese Tasters
Nairn's cheese oatcakes
Ritz Bits Sandwiches
Quavers
Crunchy Cheetos
Flamin' Hot Cheetos
Tesco Cheese Savouries

Three is the magic number

If you search for 'grazing boards' on Pinterest, you will summon many planks teeming with garden peas, leaf-on radishes, salami slices arranged in the shape of roses, and logs of goat's cheese with edible flowers pressed into the top. You'll get brunch boards, chocolate boards, Lion King boards, taco boards and pavlova boards, and you'll see that sometimes people put cupcakes on cheeseboards to be jolly. The board cookbooks (there are many) mimic the pins and the overall sentiment of Too Much Really, and they go absolutely hell for leather on script font.

This is a trend that will not have captured your imagination if you're easily overwhelmed – and if you're not stinking rich. Of course it's 'easy' to 'throw together' a board of charcuterie, fruit, pickles, cheeses, herbs, nuts, dips and spreads if your pockets are very deep and you don't mind taking a week off work to tackle your shopping list. I love an edible spectacle as much as the next snack fan but this isn't the kind of thing I'd be able to pull off without panic, so it's just not the kind of thing I'd try to pull off.

And I'm not saying that if someone served me this sort of lollapalooza I wouldn't be delighted. I'm just saying, I can't personally get into this style of catering. First, I'd have to buy a large piece of wood and find a place for it to live. And then, when it turned out that the grand total of recipes in this book was only enough to fill one plank, I'd have to live with the guilt of leaving you all short-changed.

Plus, this serving style contravenes a feeling about cheese I've been maturing for a few years, which is that despite my tendency to want more of everything, all the time, three is the right number of cheeses for me to have access to at once. Not because more is too many, but because when you have the right three, you get a blissful, top-to-toe, bespoke cheese adventure. You get the same feeling of being looked after that you get in an aromatherapy yin yoga class when the teacher puts an eyebag on you. To receive a curated plate of three cheeses is to understand that a professional has taken care of things, channelling their years of know-how into one good thing for you to revel in.

I love to experience this dining alchemy and tend not to be hugely interested in learning to perform it myself. I don't generally condone living in ignorance so that you might (if you are white, and especially if you are also male) experience life as a type of magic, but I think it's OK to apply this approach to cheese. So, if I was serving cheese at home, I'd just ask the cheesemonger what to do, keeping my shimmering cloak of cluelessness fastened securely around me. I'd tell her I needed three cheeses to surprise and delight. That I love the sultry, supple ones – your Sainte-Nectaires and your Mont d'Ors. And that my favourite hard cheese is Coolea, an Irish one that tastes like hazelnuts and butterscotch. I'd be pretty confident in that as a brief, but realistically my nearest cheesemonger is 45 minutes away and I have 3,000 words to write, a birthday dinner to prep and a will to sign by the end of the week – I'm not going to make it to the cheesemonger. So, in the real world, what would I do? Without troubling myself to learn too much about the finer details of the world's 1,500(-ish) cheeses, how would I choose a melodious trio?

First, there's a list I love in Anne Saxelby's *The New Rules of Cheese*. It's a list of 'failsafe' options to buy from supermarkets and it includes aged Gouda, Manchego, Gruyère, sharp Cheddar and Parmigiano Reggiano. So that's your hard cheese taken care of. And after that, all that matters is variety. We know in our hearts that we probably want cheeses across the categories (fresh, hard, soft, aged, blue), with different textures, strengths, flavour profiles and perhaps animal origins (cow, sheep, goat). But if the thought of trying to tick all those boxes makes you want to get a nice Boursin and be done with it (also fine), know that we can get the result we're after simply by going for three cheeses that look different – by letting shape and colour show us the way. One honey-coloured slab, one grey pyramid, one oozing, creamy wedge.

To serve, the classic cheese books recommend a large piece of slate or wood, or a marble slab, festooned with vine leaves, chestnut leaves or wild flowers (whatever you 'happen' to have 'on hand'), plus figs, apricots, dates, nuts and all that claptrap. Sound familiar? I guess the dark art of plank arrangement isn't so new. If I've convinced you of the merits of a three-step cheese adventure then I reckon little chunks on individual plates (paper ones, even!) is the way to do it, aiming for around 60g of cheese per person (definitely taken out of the fridge an hour before you want to eat it). Then, you just need bread and/or crackers, and a few of your favourite condiments (mine are on page 118 and page 215).

Finally, I enjoy this hot tip from Michel Roux's *Cheese*. He says that if he had four people to feed, his 'advice would be to serve just one generous wedge of perfectly ripe cheese'. And I think in the right scenario I would be willing to overlook my rule of three for one absolute humdinger, because I would really like to be the sort of person who casually offers her dear pals slivers from an entire wheel of cheese. Oh, Laura Goodman? Yeah, she's always got a wheel 'on hand'. Meagre supply of chestnut leaves, though.

Anyway, I've already learned too much. I need to leave it here, before I start to understand the difference between a washed rind and a bloomy one. My cloak is slipping – I think I just dragged the feather trim through the mud. Urgh, I hate it when that happens. Over to the expert.

Some cheese trios generously suggested by Dan Bliss, cheese buyer at London's magical old cheesemongers, Paxton & Whitfield:

Three for Laura (based on my 'brief' above)
Old Groendal
Maida Vale
Granizo Trufado

Most snackable
'I love a "session cheese" – something you can go back to again and again. Plus, all of these cheeses are amazing with a slice of apple':
Gorwydd Caerphilly
Tunworth
Ashcombe

English
Montgomery Cheddar
Stichelton
Baron Bigod

Alpine
Mont d'Or
Comté (around 18 months old ideally)
Tomme de Savoie

Great with champagne
Langres
Parmigiano Reggiano
Ticklemore goat's cheese

Soft and decadent

Gorgonzola Dolce

Brillat-Savarin

Canarejal Cremoso

To cut a Langres story short . . .

I know I said I wasn't interested in alchemy, but here's some amateur fizzy business for your table. It turns out that Langres – a silky, rich little drum with a wrinkly orange rind – has an intentional dip in the top (it's never flipped while it's maturing, unlike other, similar cheeses). And that dip is – *naturellement* – best used as a reservoir for a splash of champagne. You just slosh it in and get your friends to watch your cash bubble into a meaningless but fantastic frenzy, and then you eat it.

Life's better with feta

A deeply tedious thing I am wont to do is ask you which three cheeses you'd choose if you knew you only had access to three forever. You'll start off thinking big; you might throw words like BRIE DE MEAUX and MANCHEGO in my face, but then you'll realise: *she said forever.* So you'll want Parmesan for your pasta and Cheddar because it's your lifeblood. And then – what would a Friday night be without mozzarella? And lo, you'll end up with three cheeses from a popular pool of about five. I see you. I invented this game. You cannot outsmart me.

I'm not going to tell you my three here because despite my giving it the biggun, I'm not confident enough to commit them to paper. But what I will tell you is that I always choose feta. Here is a cheese that is capable of giving pizzazz to a tomato risotto, a black bean taco, a slow-cooked lamb shoulder *and* a roasted squash. So yes, the versatility of feta gives it a special place in my heart and my fridge, until it takes on the smell of old dishcloths. And if you think of feta as a crumbly, briny bitpart in your life that's not up to anything more strenuous than a half-arsed smattering, I'd only ask that you eat a Greek salad or a spanakopita with a glass of white wine on a sunny day and get back to me.

But everyone knows that the cheeses with true star quality are the ones you can put in the oven, whole. And look, I'm not going to pretend that a baked feta can provide the same sense of occasion as a baked Vacherin, which – with its task force of potatoes and cornichons – is quite literally the crème de la crème of hot cheese. But feta has its own thing going on.

You could serve a baked feta with the fresh friends you're accustomed to seeing it with – lots of lemony peppers, tomatoes, parsley and olives. Or, you could serve it in a more regal style, topped with a sticky bronze crown of clustered nuts. This recipe is categorical evidence that feta can be a showpiece, too.

Honey-nut baked feta

Serves 2–4

1 x 200g block of feta
1 tablespoon olive oil

70g hazelnuts
1½ tablespoons sesame seeds
5 tablespoons honey
a few picked thyme leaves
crackers, to serve

1. Preheat the oven to 200°C/180°C fan/gas 6.

2. Rest the feta in a small roasting dish and drizzle with the olive oil. Bake for 25 minutes or until starting to brown at the edges – it helps to give it a little baste half-way through.

3. Meanwhile, toast the hazelnuts and sesame seeds in a small frying pan until golden and smelling nutty. Turn the heat off.

4. Only once the feta has finished baking (because it needs a few minutes to chill out), add the honey and thyme leaves to the frying pan with the nuts, turn the heat back on, and let it all bubble for a couple of minutes, swirling the pan.

5. Pour over the feta, and serve with the crackers.

Frico croccante

Do something crazy today. Take a big pinch of finely grated mature Cheddar, Parmesan or pecorino Romano, and drop it on a hot frying pan. First, the little mound will melt down into a puddle like the Wicked Witch of the West and then it will start to bubble. Very soon, it will be nothing but bubbles and you'll doubt that it's ever going to amount to anything. After a while, as the bubbling eases, the cheese will start to look like it's going to form something cohesive, but it's still sticky, so don't touch it yet (never touch it with your fingertips, because it's hotter than hell). Once a stillness has descended, you must flip it, but only for a few seconds. Lift it out with a spatula. It's bendy now, but over the next 27 seconds, it will cool to a crisp.

I hope everybody likes a cheeseball!

In season one episode two of *Schitts Creek*, we have not yet taken the Roses into our hearts and tucked them there forever. We have absolutely no idea how much crying lies ahead of us, or how much humanity it's possible to pour into an 18-minute episode. It still just seems like something fun and silly to put on when you feel like an empty potato sack. And it is! Because in the same way that life steals all your potatoes, life is the funnest, silliest thing of all.

In the previous episode we met the Rose family and we saw them get evicted from their grand old home. We heard that the one asset the government had allowed them to retain was a town Johnny once bought David for a joke ('The joke was owning the town! That was the joke!'). We saw them schlep their overblown belongings to a motel that smelled 'like a gym bag' in the joke town. That episode set us up, but in episode two, we start to get into it. What is this schitty creek like? What kind of folks are here? How will this money-mad (awful?) family fit in?

At this point, the Roses are still toying with a clutch of highly tenuous routes out. Acceptance hasn't come yet. Alexis thinks 'Stavros' is coming to get her (and only her) but he decides to go to Diddy's white party instead. Johnny is fixated on getting his deeds signed by Roland Schitt, the mayor, so that he can put the town on the market and bust out of there. Roland knows no one is going to buy it but invites (or forces) the Roses to dinner at his house so he can sign them anyway.

It's at the Schitt home that a cheeseball is unveiled – by Jocelyn, Roland's wife: 'I hope everybody likes a cheese-ball!' she says, without self-consciousness. 'It's the treat that keeps our love life percolating.' The cheeseball is a large, nut-covered orb around which the dynamic is arranged. It's a symbol of where the Roses find themselves and how horrifying that is to them right now. When Johnny takes a cracker to it, the ball does not relent. The cracker snaps. And then, while the Roses sneer at the impenetrable sphere, Jocelyn asks, with kindness, about David's career as a gallerist. Obviously, David can't be bothered to engage with small-town folk about his highfalutin life, but he offers them a crumb: his gallery used to work with Janet Kempfluugen.

. . .

He drops the name in the way that people do when they expect you to know their world inside out but couldn't give two shits about yours. To two blank Schitt faces, he explains: 'She would walk into the space wearing a clay mask of a fawn, remove her clothing and breastfeed members of the audience. It was a commentary on income inequality.'

And it's clear: Jocelyn is not the joke. The Schitts are not the joke. This small town that happens to be the Roses' only refuge is not the joke, and neither is the cheeseball.

I'm not from a culture of cheeseballs (triangles, yes) but (as I'm sure you will have gathered by now) I studied Media Studies at A-Level, so I have always understood what they represent: something low, something to pour scorn on. After all, no true connoisseur of cheese would roll it into a ball. We take care to brew our coffee in AeroPresses and finish everything we make, sweet or savoury, with a flurry of Maldon sea salt, so as if we'd be seen dead rolling cheese into balls. There's just no way anyone's doing that *chez Kempfluugen*.

And yet when I saw that cracker succumbing to Jocelyn's hard ball, I knew I needed more balled cheese in my life. I ordered what is now one of my favourite books: *Great Balls of Cheese*, by Michelle Buffardi. On the cover is a soft cheese owl, with plumes of flaked almond feathers, carved carrot feet and the kindest black olive eyes. And inside there are 'more than 50 irresistible cheese ball creations for any occasion'.

There's a caterpillar made up of multiple herb-coated balls arranged in a wiggle. There's a Christmas tree covered with parsley pine needles, studded with pomegranate baubles and topped with a pear star. And there's a pimiento cheese chick with a perfect almond beak. The nacho cat is Kempfluugen tier art: she has ginger carrot stripes, chive whiskers, and nacho ears. And she sounds delicious, too.

And that's the thing – these balls all sound good. The beer-pretzel ball is loaded with Cheddar, shallots, ale and hot sauce, and covered with crushed pretzels. And the lox bagel ball just makes sense – it's a one-ball wonder of cream cheese, smoked salmon, spring onion and capers.

At the heart of every cheeseball in *Great Balls* is cream cheese. And to that you might add other soft cheeses or grated hard cheeses and any number of genius mix-ins. At the end, you roll the cheese ball in its coating, which might be nuts, seeds, crushed crackers or herbs. A word of warning from Buffardi: 'If you're bringing a cheeseball to a party, keep the ball and the coating in separate containers and assemble just before serving.' Dedicate yourself to this snack, please.

Jocelyn clearly worked hard on her cheeseball (and the rest of dinner) for people we all knew wouldn't appreciate it (and for her husband, who does appreciate it, and who she loves in spite of the way he uses a whole hand to rummage in the communal fondue). But why was her cheeseball so hard? She overloaded it? She chilled it too enthusiastically? Or it wasn't really a cheeseball at all, but a gesture of open arms and a comic device (I got an A).

In the introduction to *Great Balls*, Buffardi says:

'Somewhere along the way, "cheese ball" became associated with the "uncool" – a term reserved for bad jokes, ugly gifts that beg to be regifted, or hideous patterns on a tablecloth or skirt. But the appetizer that is literally a ball of cheese deserves much more respect.'

In season one episode two, the Roses do not respect the cheeseball, or its providers. They still need to be exposed to a lot of love before their nutty outer shells will start to relent to the many crackers of the Creek. But what is amazing is the way they are all so instantly themselves. David is perfectly, phenomenally scathing and Alexis describes the motel as 'cute' and the diner as 'kind of sweet' while plotting never to eat or sleep in them again. Johnny tries to rally the troops and get a handle on things, while palpably losing it ('This place is a dump, it's a dump, you know what? It's a hellhole!'), and Moira keeps busy with her wigs and her special brand of melodrama ('In hell, there's no bellman'). As we rattle through the episodes, these characters do not become different people to accommodate the plot; they are there all along, four hardballs softening up, episode by episode.

Over six seasons, they teach us how to leave judgement at the door. This show, which seems to have a knack for finding people when they need it most, is packed with more delight, empathy, kindness and jokes than I can comprehend, multiple re-watches later. And this is the sort of table I want to set, too – a judgement-free zone, filled with delight, empathy, kindness and jokes. So, it makes sense that I'd want to put a cheeseball in the middle of it.

Look, there's no cheeseball at David and Patrick's wedding as far as I can see – that would make this protracted metaphor so neat that someone else would've written about it already. But we don't get to go to the reception, do we? So let's imagine. What if Jocelyn rolled her most spectacular cheeseball yet? What if it was in the shape of a love heart?

Or Mariah Carey? What if she took it to the venue in two separate containers – one for the ball and one for the coating? You just know that when they arrived, sodden with tears and shimmering with love, Moira, Johnny, David and Alexis grabbed a cracker apiece, without thinking twice.

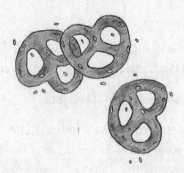

Honey, mustard and onion cheeseball

Leave your judgement at the door, then, and let's roll. Here's a recipe for a cheeseball – not a joke, but a great snack which happens to be spherical. Clearly, I owe Michelle Buffardi everything for this. But inspiration comes from all around and as such I also drew from one of my favourite packet snacks: Snyder's Honey, Mustard and Onion Pretzel Pieces. The resulting cheeseball is a savoury fandango, smothered with pretzels. It's a gesture of open arms, a thank you for being here, and a delicious centrepiece for your snackfest.

Serves 6

180g cream cheese
¼ shallot, very finely chopped

1 tablespoon wholegrain mustard

2 teaspoons honey

1 teaspoon Worcestershire sauce

50g Cheddar, finely grated

45g salted pretzels, crushed (and lots more whole pretzels to serve)

1. Beat together the cream cheese, shallot, mustard, honey and Worcestershire sauce until even and smooth.

2. Mix through the grated Cheddar.

3. Pat and roll the cheese mix into a rough ball – it might feel a bit wetter and looser than other things you've balled in your lifetime, but you'll be surprised how nicely it shapes up. Chill it in the fridge for at least 2 hours.

4. On a dinner plate, roll the ball of cheese in the crushed pretzel coating just before serving.

COVID diaries: a labneh story

LOCKDOWN 1

My friend Laura is not long back from LA. While she was there, she sent me a video tour of her cabin in Topanga Canyon. This place I'd never been – essentially a treehouse above all of southern California, with VIP access to the sky, eyes on the ocean and easy access by comfortable American car to the Silverlake branch of Intelligentsia coffee shop – has become for me, my number one lockdown fantasy. But I will not dig out Laura's video to torture myself.

I am forever pining for California. I have always had this feeling of homesickness from LA despite having never lived there. I wonder when I will be reunited with my heart? I wonder when I will smell the warm, cinnamony tarmac of LAX again? I wonder when I will bathe in a gloopy orange sunset from the passenger seat of a large hire car again? It's not pining this time; it's something new.

LOCKDOWN 2

When Laura got back from that LA trip it was my birthday and we were supposed to go to Ducksoup in Soho but I had a cough, and this coronavirus thing was getting weird, so we didn't go. And isn't it *just so pandemic* that Ducksoup, 19 minutes away on the tube, is now as much of a fantasy as Topanga Canyon, actual heaven.

At Ducksoup I liked to sit at the bar, or if I happened to be in a three, right up in the crook of the little window, eyes on Dean Street. I remember always wanting to order the labneh, but feeling that it might be a waste to order it again – a waste of money? Appetite? I'm not sure. I just recall feeling that I should try something else. But the balls of labneh *were* the bar; they sat on it and they inhabited it. In their wooden barrel, they bathed in herby olive oil, waiting for me. This is the magic of restaurants I can scarcely remember: their readiness.

In the future, all being well, I will never not order the labneh at Ducksoup. I will always be earlier than Laura (that bit won't be hard) (just kidding Laura) (not really kidding at all) so that I can sit there and think about what I've done, which is taken the tube for 19 minutes, walked among very many people, climbed atop a stool that is a little uncomfortably high for me to tell the truth, and ordered the bloody labneh.

LATER

When I got to Ducksoup I saw someone I knew from the internet sitting out the front with a glass of grenache. Recently, this was unimaginable and now, here I am, tripping off the curb to say hello. I was earlier than Laura, but not much, and they don't serve the labneh in balls now, but in a sort of smear. I couldn't read the wine list because the lockdowns have ruined my eyesight. We shared five great plates, including the labneh. Laura said: 'It's just good, isn't it?'

Labneh: it's just good

I use the same quantities suggested in the Ducksoup cookbook (1 teaspoon of salt to 500g of yoghurt) because it's just good. Below I recommend draining the yoghurt for 3 days, but if you're not fussed about rolling it into balls and submerging it in oil, you can just drain it for 2 days and you'll get a softer spread.

Makes 15-ish balls

1 teaspoon fine sea salt
500g full-fat plain yoghurt
300ml extra virgin olive oil
10g mixed fresh dill and parsley, roughly chopped

2 teaspoons lemon zest

2 teaspoons chilli flakes

You also need

2 layers of cheesecloth (in roughly 45cm squares)

a bag clip or elastic band

a nice clean jar (I use a Mrs Elswood pickled cucumber jar, naturally)

1. Rest a sieve over a mixing bowl and line the sieve with your square of double-layered cheesecloth.

2. Mix the fine sea salt into the yoghurt using a fork and scoop the mix into the cheesecloth-lined sieve. It's a good idea to taste it now purely so you can better appreciate its radical transformation from salty yoghurt to almost-cheese.

3. Gather the edges of the cheesecloth and secure into a bundle using an elastic band or a bag clip.

4. Leave to rest like this in the fridge for 3 days. (You can leave it for 1–2 days, and it'll still be labneh, but you won't be able to ball it up.)

5. When you're ready, measure out the oil in a jug and stir through the herbs, lemon zest and chilli flakes.

6. Roll the labneh into balls (about 20g or a generous tablespoon) and place in your clean jar. It'll be sticky, so it might help to lightly oil your hands.

7. Top up the jar with the herby oil until the labneh is fully submerged (if it's not, add more oil).

8. Put the lid on and keep the jar somewhere cool for up to a month. You *can* keep it in the fridge but the oil will solidify, so you'd need to let the jar come to room temperature each time you want it.

9. When you're ready to scoop some out to eat, serve it with a pool of the herby oil and a chunk of bread.

When I was a young mozzarella

In 2013 I was working in a job I didn't believe in. I was 28 and still intimidated by men who spent all day pretending to be brilliant. I worked at a social media agency full of bean bags that had absolutely no idea what it was doing but which had been ready to monetise toilet roll tweets at exactly the right moment. I can't afford a legal read on this book so just try to imagine the bits in between while I skip straight to a dinner in Covent Garden after a long day of pure drivel at – let's call it – Visage Journal HQ. We're in the kind of restaurant that is right under your nose, which you'd find adorable if you were off to see a show with a beloved friend afterwards. But in this scenario, I'm sitting opposite a man who's done nothing but regurgitate my ideas as his own all day and is continuing the charade of pretending to be brilliant after hours.

It's 2013 but maybe you can't remember much about that year, so let's just say: Barack Obama has been inaugurated for a second term, you bob your head to Lorde's Royals as you meander around Morrisons in a trance and, on 'Netflix' – which you might only have had access to for a few months – the normally law-abiding Piper Chapman has been sentenced to a year and a half behind bars.

Burrata is yet to go mainstream in the UK. When it's on a menu, you occasionally get the sense that the person who wrote the menu doesn't know why they put it there. It's not yet being whacked in the middle of pizzas or dressed to the nines in technicolour tomatoes. You definitely can't buy it tucked lovelessly in plastic tubs from the supermarket.

As for me, my personal life is in a state of flux, I use a Babyliss Big Hair rotating brush to make waves even though I have naturally curly hair, and my friend Janet and I were recently introduced to a man called Fagioli in an old Florence cafeteria. We will quote the line 'His name . . . is Beans' hysterically forever.

Back in Covent Garden, my brilliant colleague Cara is study-ing the menu, and has just asked the table a question.

'What's burrata?'

Trying hard not to sound like a know-it-all (I am a 28-year-old woman), I say: 'I think it's . . . like . . . mozzarella with cream in the middle?'

Always the ?

The not-brilliant man opposite, let's call him James, looks straight through me and delivers a line now as immortal as Fagioli's friend's: 'A burrata is a young mozzarella.'

> *A burrata is a young mozzarella.*
> *A burrata is a young mozzarella.*
> *A burrata is a young mozzarella.*

There he is, look! Champion of garbage! Knower of no things! Strutter of mousey office floors! Loser of foosball! And of course, to this, I say nothing. James being a James, and me being a me means that I'm not sure now – what if burrata comes to hold cream as a result of an ageing process? I didn't think mozzarella had a lot to do with ageing (being a fresh cheese), but what if it does? What if I'm wrong? I'd want to have my facts straight before presenting them as gospel, wouldn't I?

Fact check, then. Burrata takes the same stretched curds that mozzarella is made from and uses them as a casing for stracciatella, which is the frayed edges of more stretched curds, mixed with cream. Or, to put it bluntly, it's mozzarella with cream in the middle. No question mark.

Of course, I have versions of this conversation every week. Because unlike James, I can't say in a meeting, with a straight face: 'this is a future truth' or 'this is my Eiffel Tower moment' or 'let's do some north-star-type thinking' when I know those statements to be devoid of meaning. But next time you're caught feeling rattled by a moron, if you can't find the conviction or energy to defend your position, perhaps it will at least bring levity to the situation and break the cycle of despair and frustration if you draw for these words: *burrata is a young mozzarella*. And later, when you're able to verify that you were right all along, simply send your James the appropriate Wikipedia link, or balls and balls of very old mozzarella.

Burrata with orange and pistachios

If and when you do treat yourself to a loveless plastic tub, you owe it to the squishy, rapidly deteriorating ball of cream within (eat it ASAP) to do something more than dump it on a plate. Not much more, though. There are lots of lovely, elaborate saladly ideas out there; this is just a quick route to a perfectly ceremonious snack.

Serves 2

1 tablespoon extra virgin olive oil
1 tablespoon orange juice
finely grated zest of ½ orange
1 teaspoon balsamic vinegar
fine sea salt
black pepper
1 x 100g burrata
10g salted pistachios, chopped

1. Mix the oil, juice, zest, vinegar, a pinch of salt and a few twists of black pepper, or shake them up in an old jar.

2. Put the burrata on a plate and cut a little cross in it to open it up a bit, before spooning the dressing over, and sprinkling with the chopped nuts.

Tiny cheese biscuits

Lots of us made cheese biscuits like these as kids, but why did we stop? The basic formula is so easy that even adults can remember it (100g each of butter, flour and cheese – it's based on a Simon Hopkinson recipe, as so many good things are). The sesame seeds, mustard powder and cayenne are there for crunch, oomph and heat respectively, but you could easily drop any of those if you don't have them. These are cheesy, crumbly, one-bite wonders – snackable in the extreme. If they do make it to a plate, they'll fly right off it.

Makes 50–60

100g unsalted butter, cold and cubed
100g plain flour
100g Cheddar cheese, finely grated (and a bit extra)
2 teaspoons sesame seeds
1 teaspoon mustard powder
a pinch of fine sea salt
a pinch of cayenne
1 egg

1. To make the dough in a food processor, pulse all the ingredients until they come together, and skip to 3.

2. To make by hand, rub together the butter and flour until you have fine breadcrumbs which seem interested in forming clumps. Then toss the cheese, sesame seeds, mustard powder, salt and cayenne through with your hands until evenly dispersed.

3. Now work the mix together into a smooth ball – you won't need any water or egg.

4. Leave it in the fridge for an hour.

5. Heat the oven to 180°C/160°C fan/gas 4, and line two baking trays.

6. Roll the dough out to about ½cm thickness. I like to cut mine into 3cm squares with a knife, but you can also go for circles, stars, whatever you like.

7. Transfer the cut biscuits to your trays.

8. Give your egg a little mix with a fork in a mug and use it to brush each biscuit. Add an extra sprinkle of cheese to the tops.

9. Bake for about 14 minutes, until they're nice and golden and the whole house smells cheesy.

Ritz o' clock: how to do the most with a box of Ritz crackers

It was 2007 and we were running out of money on Bondi Beach. The promising hostel with the roof terrace had turned out to be a dump, of course. For dinner on the dump's steaming summit, we had at our disposal: a box of Ritz crackers, a packet of cream cheese and the end of a jar of green olives. I probably don't need to spell out how we Ready Steady Cooked those three ingredients, but I'm going to anyway: we constructed delicate little stacks on repeat until the box was empty, and we laughed our heads off thinking about the lavish, sun-drenched meals we'd imagined we might eat on Bondi Beach.

I think what was making us hysterical, though, was (yes, the untethered deliciousness of being in our twenties, but also) the way we were cutting our rubbish little olives in half to garnish each cracker. We were making this basic snack (which I now know to be a popular one in the under-threes community) into something semi-civilised. And we were having the time of our lives doing it.

I am still a little obsessed with Ritz crackers. I love the audacity and nostalgia of the red box – all those little crackers cutting loose in there, without a plastic tray to hold them in place. The crackers themselves are delicious, sturdy and kind of beautiful in their special scallopy way.

I've always liked the idea of pre-making a lot of little Ritz canapés and setting them out on the table, but – for me – a more realistic approach is to put a few boxes on the table and let people get to work. I'm in my thirties now, so it makes perfect sense that if I want to go on an adventure with a box of Ritz crackers, I add an additional topping to the Bondi model – one for each decade lived.

So what I've created for you below is a little Ritz matrix. Each cracker can have a cheese, a thing that isn't cheese and a garnish, and you can just let everyone mix and match. I'm trying to sound relaxed as I type that but I know you can feel my Monica Geller energy seeping between the commas. I'm thinking of all the crackers inevitably leaving the table with only one topping.

For pudding Ritzes, half dip the crackers in dark or white chocolate and decorate them with sprinkles. Then, please only serve these if everyone has eaten the savoury ones in the manner I have illustrated.

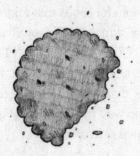

Cheeses
Feta
Cream cheese
Cheddar, sliced or cut into Ritz-sized circles
Ricotta
Spreadable goat's cheese

Things that aren't cheese
Smoked salmon
Salami slices (conveniently circular)
Avocado
Chilli jam
Tapenade

Garnishes
Halved grapes
Sliced cucumber
Pickled red onions
Cornichons
Olives

Have you considered a condiment?

At one point, we had so many condiments in our fridge that we did not have room for foods that might actually sustain us, so Rich made a sign for the door. It screamed: 'HAVE YOU CONSIDERED A CONDIMENT?' Each time we opened the fridge, he reasoned, we'd be forced to contemplate the jarscape that was our own terrifying creation. Until – in the same way that we'd stopped seeing most of the jars – we stopped seeing the sign.

Honestly, condiments: where does it end? You could just keep popping them into your basket with an innocent 'ooh' forever and ever. You could and I will. The ones I've listed below are snackers' condiments – not necessarily magic sauces to elevate your cooking, but reliable companions to boost the plate in front of you, whatever happens to be on it.

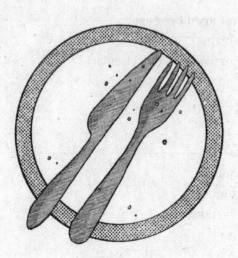

Chaat masala

Snacker's delight.

Ballymaloe Original Relish

One of my most-used, this turns a lump of Cheddar or a single cold sausage into something I can really get behind.

Encona Original Hot Pepper Sauce

I find the hot sauce market frankly overwhelming, but I love the formula of this one such that it gets used up and rebought while its rivals solidify at the bottleneck.

Fage Total 0% Greek yoghurt

Do I, in fact, have any idea what a condiment is? Maybe, maybe not. All I know is that a crushed or minced clove of garlic and a squeeze of lemon in thick Greek yoghurt is my . . . jam.

Maille Dijon Mustard

Imagine *not* having it.

Edmund Fallot Tarragon Dijon Mustard

This is my favourite condiment for making things taste like you've done something complicated when you've done nothing, and for leftover roast chicken sandwiches.

Colman's English Mustard

Which you could mix with a little of the below for a lazy devilled egg.

Hellmann's Real Mayonnaise

Those hell men just know what they're doing.

Hellmann's Vegan Mayo

They

Just

Know!

Mrs Elswood Haimisha Cucumbers

My best friends.

Those little jars of cornichons with mini onions

Aw. I admit they're altogether cuter, crunchier and more satisfying to eat with cheese and cured meat than my best friends above.

Geeta's Premium Lime Pickle

I eat this more with Cheddar cheese than I do with dinner at this point.

Geeta's Premium Mango Chutney

I'm not the kind of fanatic who regularly spoons this straight into my mouth, but I also couldn't imagine life without the option to do so.

Geeta's Premium Aubergine Pickle

You might as well just work your way through the range and see what sticks. For me, this.

Fortnum & Mason Piccadilly Piccalilli

I was slow to adopt. I always felt like it was doing too much, with the saturation turned up too high. How could something be that yellow? How could it be mustardy and pickly at the same time? Why would I want it to be? Because it's great.

Nigella's chilli jam
You can't buy this but you should add it to your list of Chrismukkah traditions.

Kikkoman Soy Sauce (1L)
I just enjoy having a massive bottle of soy sauce to wield while I ask anyone I can force to listen: 'Do you think I've got enough soy sauce?' If you've got space, what could be a saltier, handier item to call your own?

Basra Date Syrup
It's so dark, thick, glossy, sweet and good, especially on a blank canvas of Greek yoghurt.

Apricot jam
For life and for halloumi (thank you, Georgie Hayden).

Fig jam
For cheese. I have no brand preference but I tend to favour packaging that features the word fig in Italian because I'm an idiot (*fichi*).

Peanut butter
I wouldn't be a geriatric millennial without it!

Al Nakhil Tahina Extra
I love the tahini that trickles. This one comes from Lebanon in pleasing tahini-coloured plastic tubs with green lids, or – if you're really lucky – buckets.

Lao Gan Ma Crispy Chilli in Oil
This can make plain rice and steamed fish something you actually want to eat, so imagine what it can do to your snacks.

Yonca Pickled Jalapeños (the sliced ones)

It would be impossible to evoke ballpark shenanigans without them (nachos and hot dogs).

LIFE SNACKS IV (misc)

- A crab sandwich eaten pregnantly on a rock in Newlyn, Cornwall, despite vague concerns about ingesting too much mercury.

- A green chicken tamale with a cafe con leche.

- A box of Cheezels in a hotel room on New Year's Eve in Melbourne.

- A strawberry and whipped cream sando on milk bread from a 7-Eleven in Tokyo.

- In Tulum, you had to flash a light on the pitch black strip to get a taxi to take you to town. There, just off the main square, where an outdoor dance class was a cross-generational fandango and the air smelled of cinnamon sugar, we found panuchos – fried corn tortillas stuffed with refried beans. They were served on the pavement by a couple who'd driven for hours with their complex network of Tupperwares, containing salsas, braises and shredded bits and bobs. We sat on plastic chairs and drank massive Cokes.

- Restorative chips and scraps in Scarborough after a knickerbocker glory threatened to send me into a chasmic slump.

- A ribeye and cheese taco with a bottle of Modelo.

- Rich's home fries, straight from the pan.

- Sweet chilli coated peanuts at my friend Kate's tiny flat in Islington. She had a foldaway cupboard for a kitchen, which was fine because we were both heartbroken and eating badly. There was no dinner to ruin by eating too many coated peanuts, and that was something.

- Chicken patties from Juici Patties in Jamaica, a chain whose rivalry with Tastee Patties is legendary (we didn't get to the latter). On the same unforgettable roadtrip, we also pulled into a YAM STOP for a buttered yam wrapped in foil.

- My friend Tillie's cinnamon buns, especially the time we all rallied to toast the hazelnuts and mix the cream cheese drizzle the morning after a sleepover when she inexplicably lived in a small town famous for battle reenactments.

A CUP OF COFFEE

Choose your fighter

People worry about losing their edge when they become parents – having nothing interesting to say, becoming a cliché. And let me tell you: they grow up so fast, I feel as though I might die of love, my hair is in a perpetual bun and yes (absolutely, 100%, it couldn't be truer), I live for my morning cup of coffee.

The smell of it, the feel of the mug warm on my clutching palm, the heat, the steam, the darkness, the slug of oat milk, the fug-clearing first sip. Coffee is my favourite bit of any holiday, and coffee itself feels like a small holiday every morning. Despite drinking most of my coffee at home, I still find that it transports me – somewhere I've been a million times or somewhere I've never been in my life. A flapping bit of canvas in a chilly camp in Yosemite National Park the morning after a campfire, a wobbly chair on a cobbled piazza in Sicily, a bouncy red booth in a diner in Houston, Texas (baby), an organic solid wood table in a café in Copenhagen, a heavy-duty Thermos on a hiking trail in the Lake District, feet dangling from the edge of one of Saturn's moons on a clear spring morning. Chop chop, drink up (or decant your coffee into your travel cup), we're late for the childminder.

We have all had to get better at living moment to moment in recent years and coffee represents one of the most important daily moments for so many of us. I want you to embrace your moment and get the most from it – give yourself a little extra so that you can really linger on your moon, or at your nan's flat in the 1990s, or with a beautifully sculpted lifeguard on Bondi Beach, wherever it may be.

There's an Instagram account which is supposed to be about Parisians wearing outfits, but to me is about Parisians being in Paris. I don't often wear Breton stripes for reasons to do with my pathetic determination to be an individual, but I was so drawn to this photo of a woman in comfy slip-ons, loose jeans and a Breton top. It was just an outfit that she was living in, and she looked – to me – to be really living, because she was striding past a pavement café. She was probably just walking to the office, but the picture reminded me of a feeling – the one you get when you find your stride in another place, when you find a small way of making it yours, a feeling I've had in Paris. A feeling that usually starts with coffee.

In Paris I've always tended to get up and amble around the same neighbourhood – from snack to snack, crêpe to eclair, Sephora to kir royale. Turns out, that was the correct approach. This isn't something that happens to me very often (I usually think all the things I've ever done are stupid and wrong), but it turns out that in Paris, I was doing it right! I was footloose, living in a world in which international travel was easy, without any work to do or children to put shoes on, so of course I never swallowed up full days with gallery bookings. Time to drift, time to take it all in, time to hang out with people I love.

Let's bring a little of that energy to our everyday lives. Take a minute to dream up the most *you* mug possible (individuate at all costs) and then make that mug happen (am I writing a meditation?). Do whatever it takes to get that mug into your cupboard and your life. This is a dream you can have come true over and over again, every morning. For me, it's a cream-coloured diner mug with chunky sides which is also quite dinky so that I can cradle those walls with my whole hand and I can keep topping myself up over the course of the morning. And because what's on the outside does count, it has a flamingo on it, and the word *Florida* in swirly vintage type. I bought it, not in Florida, where I have hardly been, but on eBay for £3.80 + P&P. Three hundred and eighty pence of unadulterated one-legged birdy delight.

Once you've got the mug, you're ready for the snack. The one you eat when it's finally just you, your cafetière and your computer, or the one you sneak when the kids are hopped up on Weetabix playing in the sandpit, or the one you baked specially because your friend is coming 'for coffee' and you're as giddy as if you were 11 and Anita was coming over to play Mastermind.

In my previous book I wrote a recipe for 'breakfast cake', one of my favourites I've written because it fulfilled an important brief I'd set myself about determining what makes a cake right for 8 a.m. The answer, I decided: buttermilk. It makes a sunny, golden cake that takes its cues from a fluffy stack of pancakes, with its slight tang and tender softness. The bit of the graph where cake and breakfast intersect has always been my zone.

But some people drink coffee when it's not the morning! So maybe it's late and the coffee's in your flask with a glug of Baileys and the snack is wrapped in foil in your pocket, melting just a bit. Rarely have I felt as alive as the few times in Hollywood that Rich and I chose to go – after dinner – to the diner down the road for two mugs of coffee and one slice of cherry pie, caffeine-fuelled shenanigans glowing sweetly under strip lights.

For us, coffee's most ardent followers, a mug of coffee is this great homing beacon, the punctuation mark that helps us unpickle ourselves, detangling yesterday's business from today's. It's a comfort, a prize, a necessity and a joy, and when something means a lot to you, it's worth paying attention to it. What happens when you let your coffee light your path? Where will your dream mug take you today? Like grown-up Augustus Gloops, let us fall bun-first into the ambrosial coffee river that flows through this sweet, creamy, crumbly chapter.

The plain cake with the sweet brown crumbs on the top

In case you don't know, let me bring you up to speed: there is a type of coffee cake that doesn't contain coffee – it's a cake that has been designed (painstakingly, as it turns out) to *go* with coffee. This kind of coffee cake is snacked on widely in the coffee shops of the USA and in The Suicide episode of *Seinfeld*. In this (deeply problematic, occasionally unwatchable, don't even talk to me about Jerry's stand-up) episode, Jerry's neighbour Martin is in a little coma, so Jerry takes the opportunity to have a fling with Martin's girlfriend, Gina. Jerry and Gina bond in the hallway over Drake's Coffee Cake.

JERRY: Gina, do you know what a Drake's Coffee Cake is?

GINA: Of course, the plain cake with the sweet brown crumbs on the top.

Drake's Coffee Cakes come individually wrapped in boxes of eight (freshness guaranteed) from the supermarket (to this day). In this episode, a Drake's Coffee Cake is the mesmerically delicious, fragile, crumbly (and yet, curiously, very readily available) nucleus around which the signature (Larry) Davidian farce is choreographed. George goes to see a psychic who has a plate of Drake's Coffee Cakes at the ready when she tells him not to go to the Cayman Islands, Elaine screws up a three-day fast (for an 'ulcer test') because she finds herself in the same room as an irresistible

Drake's Coffee Cake, and Jerry uses Drake's Coffee Cake to bribe Newman not to tell Martin about his affair with Gina.

NEWMAN: . . . Is that a . . .
JERRY: Drake's Coffee Cake.
NEWMAN: Wow, where did you get that?
JERRY: From my house. I got a whole box of them.
NEWMAN: Boy, that's the full size.
JERRY: That's your big boy.
NEWMAN: Can I have a bite?
JERRY: I don't give out bites. I got another one. But I'm saving it for later.
NEWMAN: Just one bite?
JERRY: I don't think so. You know, they – they're so fragile.
NEWMAN: All right! All right. I won't say anything.
JERRY: You swear?
NEWMAN: I swear.
JERRY: On your mother's life?
NEWMAN: On my mother's life.

We know the coffee cake is fragile, plain and crumb-topped. It's so simple, and yet the characters in *Seinfeld* have a difficult time comprehending how and why it tastes as good as it does. This is the wonder of 'plain' cake – cake that might in fact contain hazelnutty browned butter, caramelly brown sugar, warm nutmeg or cinnamon, vanilla by the *table*-spoon, yoghurty tang or the richness of many egg yolks. This is why, faced with 34 flavours of cheesecake at the

Cheesecake Factory, I will go for Original (with a Freshly Brewed Coffee).

Is unapologetic a better word than plain? No concealing the cake's inherent cakiness with elderflower or raspberry or carrots. Cake for coffee must be brasher than a cake you might eat with your tea – it should be the cakiest manifestation of cake, served in hectic, tumbling slabs.

There is a formula for the perfect coffee cake and I'm not the first person to work on it – bakers were doing the sum by the 17th century. Food historians agree that the concept of eating cake with coffee started then, in Europe, though those coffee cakes are likely to have been enriched, bun-like bread snacks.

In *American Food: The Gastronomic Story*, Evan Jones explains:

'Scandinavians were perhaps more responsible than anyone else for making America as coffee-break-conscious as it is, and for perfecting the kind of food that goes well with coffee. German women had already brought the *Kaffeeklatsch* to their frontier communities, but it was in the kitchens where there was always a pot brewing on the back of the stove that Scandinavian hospitality and coffee became synonymous. There, also, began the average American's habit of having coffee with or without food, at virtually any hour of the day.'

The '*Kaffeeklatsch*', Jones explains, was a 'moment that combined gossip with coffee drinking' and it became the mid-morning or mid-afternoon equivalent of English tea-time. Help, I love it. Let's rename this book *The Big Kaffeeklatsch*. Kindly address your fanmail to my house, The Kaffeeklatsch Centre.

But anyway, Scandinavians – it all makes sense. Sweden brought us the soft, buttery cinnamon buns most of us can scarcely imagine life without, and they've also gently and quietly demonstrated to the world the concept of *fika*, as part of a healthy lifestyle that doesn't prioritise misery. Meanwhile Denmark (had you forgotten?) gave us the pastry that inhabited our coffee-drinking lives so comfortably it became known simply as: the Danish. Very slick. In the nineties, a clingfilmed box of Costco Danishes studded with ruby (raspberry) and topaz (apricot) was the surest sign you were preparing for some kind of a kaffeeklatsch, even if you didn't know it – I recall them being everywhere from my 18th birthday to my grandma's shiva.

The modern coffee cake (where the story finds us here, in the frothy wash of an oat flat white) generally features two things in abundance: a crumble or streusel topping (Gina's 'crumbs', from the German *streusen* – to sprinkle) and cinnamon (Gina's 'brown'). I am so happy to take my place at this long table of coffee-lovers hoping to find their beloved drink a crumbly, cinnamony, sweet best friend. For my part, I've thrown in cream cheese, the one true kaffeeklatsch improver of our time.

Cream cheese coffee cake

Serves 8–10

For the crumble

90g unsalted butter, cold

120g plain flour

90g light brown sugar

¼ teaspoon fine sea salt

2 teaspoons ground cinnamon

For the cake

250g plain flour

½ teaspoon fine sea salt

225g unsalted butter, softened

160g cream cheese

250g golden caster sugar

2 teaspoons vanilla extract

4 eggs

1. Preheat the oven to 160°C/140°C fan/gas 3, and butter a round 23cm cake tin.

2. First, make the crumble. In a small mixing bowl, rub the butter into the flour gently using the tips of your fingers.

3. When you have a reasonably even sandy jumble (reasonably because I like to keep some bigger buttery bits), toss the sugar, salt and cinnamon through with your hands. Set the crumble aside for now (in the fridge if you might be quite slow).

4. In a medium mixing bowl, whisk together the flour and salt, and leave to one side.

5. In a larger mixing bowl, beat the butter and cream cheese until smooth. Then add the sugar and mix until pale and fluffy – give it a good 6 minutes of your time.

6. To the butter, cream cheese and sugar, add the vanilla, then beat in the eggs one at a time. It might look a bit curdled – don't panic.

7. Use a spatula to fold the salted flour through until just combined.

8. Scrape the mix into the prepared tin and smooth the top with your spatula.

9. Sprinkle the crumble over the top – it might seem like there's loads, but don't worry – use it all up.

10. Bake for about 50 minutes, or until a skewer comes out clean.

11. Leave to cool before you slice. Serve alone, or with yoghurt and berries.

What's good with coffee? Cream and sugar

I'm not going to be moving the discussion along very much here; I have much more to say about sweet, beige, creamy, vanilla things. It was my friend Laura (now dairy intolerant) who first pointed out to me that the beige spectrum is always the sweetest spot at the ice cream shop. Totally correct, as she usually is. The ice creams, soft serves and gelati I have loved include: ricotta and honey, zabaglione, hazelnut, muscovado sugar, clotted cream, salted caramel, coconut, rice pudding, maple, cannoli and tiramisu. I would want to sneak pistachio in here, though, which is at least beige in spirit.

What these flavours amount to is mere tweaks to a smooth custard base. On a work trip to Texas I became thoroughly obsessed with exploring the concept of frozen custard. Each time I saw a sign for it, complete with neon cone and neon swirl of majestic whip, I swerved in and ordered it in its least faffed-up form – no toppings, no extras, no appendages of any kind. I wanted to know the true meaning of creamy, cold custard. Every single time, without fail, what I ordered tasted like ice cream.

This proves the difference words can make even to someone dealing in the businesses of food and words every day, because it turns out that frozen custard and ice cream really are the same thing. A frozen custard must contain eggs but in the UK every moderately fancy supermarket ice cream contains eggs anyway.

Here, I wanted to give you a silky scoop to splash with espresso or just eat with a spoon alongside a full cafetière – but I also wanted to serve you my own custard fantasy. All good custard fantasies start with Nigella and as there is almost nothing I rely on more than Nigella's basic no-churn ice cream model (except maybe my childminder, Ann-Marie), that's where I started. Next, I took the viscous, yellow, eggy weirdness that is the Dutch spirit Advocaat (she of the Snowballs) and plenty of vanilla, and my work was done: I'd created something as close to my own frozen-custard ideal as I'd ever tasted. It's ice cream, not made in an ice cream maker. It's rich, sunny custard, without fresh egg yolks. Stop trying to define her, and whisk.

No-churn frozen custard

Makes about 600ml

300ml double cream
200g condensed milk (half a tin-ish)
2 tablespoons Advocaat
2 teaspoons vanilla extract

1. Combine everything in a large bowl and whip until soft peaks form (peaks that topple when you lift the whisk, but don't disappear). You should have a smooth, airy mix that looks like pale custard and tastes like dreams.

2. Transfer the mix to a Tupperware and freeze it for at least 6 hours.

One more creamy, sugary, vanilla thing before I move on: fudge. Have you ever walked past the fudge shop on holiday and peered in as the still-warm stuff is shoved and smoothed with a paddle? Of course you have, fudge shops are positioned on cobbly crossroads so that you have no choice but to peer in. Great cauldrons of bubbling sweetness, expansive marble benches of bronze cream. I want that. I want it like that, super-fresh, supercharged; I want to be able to taste that the fudge I'm eating was only just clotted cream and sugar. And much like at the Cheesecake Factory, I don't want to happen upon bits of dried apricot, or meringue, or Dime bars.

So, the final recipe in this triptych of beige, dairy-dense, so-called plain things which taste frankly fantastic with coffee is your ticket backstage at the clotted cream fudge factory. It's yours. Make tooth marks in it. You don't even have to wait for it to cool completely if you don't want to and you can add extras at the end if you like spoiling things. And as long as you have a sugar thermometer, the method isn't even very stressful (it's not caramel, is what I'm saying). For a study in sweet, beige dairy, I recommend dicing your fudge tinily and sprinkling it on the ice cream. I recommend this so much that I cannot fathom why ice cream vans at the seaside are not doing it as standard. The fudge 99 – where is it? When will we as a people get our shit together?

Clotted cream fudge

Makes about 450g

225g clotted cream
100g golden syrup
225g light muscovado sugar
½ teaspoon sea salt flakes
1 teaspoon vanilla extract

1. Line a square 23cm tin with greaseproof paper.

2. Melt the clotted cream, golden syrup and sugar in a medium pan with high enough sides that there's plenty of room for bubbling up.

3. Stir over a medium heat until it's all melted into an even, bronze sludge, then get the sugar thermometer in position.

4. Stir occasionally until the thermometer displays 116°C, then immediately remove the pan from the heat.

5. Stir in the salt and vanilla and keep stirring for a few minutes. Suddenly the gloss will lift from the surface – that's when you want to pour it into your prepared tin.

6. Leave to cool completely, then cut into squares.

Small things that balance on saucers

My first trip with a baby was to Sicily. Each morning it seemed to take us longer to get out of our Airbnb, so we kept a stash of almond biscuits and coffee on site as a morning snack – a precursor to the main breakfast granita. There were *pasticcini di mandorle* – soft, dense, chewy, marzipanny morsels. But there were also boring old biscotti, the hard biscuits of afterthoughts.

I found myself – against all odds – preferring the latter. Biscotti are totally transformed when dipped, making them a true coffee-drinker's snack. Some professional notes: you need loads, and you need a bit of chocolate in there to melt transiently between your cup and your mouth. Start your day snacking the hard old biscuit way – you'll never look back.

Chocolate orange biscotti

Makes 30-ish pieces

100g chocolate of your choice
90g whole almonds
180g golden caster sugar
250g plain flour
1 teaspoon baking powder
½ teaspoon fine sea salt
½ teaspoon freshly grated nutmeg
finely grated zest of 2 oranges
2 eggs
2 teaspoons vanilla extract

1. Preheat the oven to 180°C/160°C fan/gas 4, and line two oven trays with baking paper.

2. Chop the chocolate into shards and small chips.

3. Roughly chop the almonds.

4. In a large mixing bowl, combine the sugar, flour, baking powder, salt, nutmeg and orange zest and mix with a wooden spoon.

5. In a smaller bowl, gently beat the eggs and vanilla with a fork.

6. Add the eggs to the dry ingredients and bring it all together to form a dough, first with the wooden spoon and then with your hands.

7. Add the chopped almonds and chocolate and work them gently through the dough with your hands.

8. Divide the dough in half and – on each of your prepared baking trays – form a slightly flattened log that's about 22cm long and doesn't taper noticeably at the ends (use plenty of flour to help with this manoeuvre if the dough is sticky).

9. Bake for about 25 minutes, until firm on the outside and golden brown.

10. Remove from the oven, then turn the oven temperature down to 150°C/130°C fan/gas 2 and leave your biscotti logs to cool for 10 minutes, before gently cutting them into 1cm slices with a bread knife (using a light sawing motion).

11. Arrange the slices on the trays and bake for 20 minutes on one side, and then 15 minutes on the other, until light brown all over.

12. Keep in an airtight container for up to 2 weeks.

Crumbly little biscuits (CLBs)

My grandma, the original stodge lover, used to bring one of three things over on a Sunday: suet pudding (which I lovingly referred to as 'sewage'), rock cakes (which Delia refers to as Good Old Rock Cakes) and *kichels*. Granny's *kichels* were not the bow-tie biscuits usually given that name. They were really just grainier, sandier, crumblier shortbread biscuits that were absolutely never uniform in shape or size (much like the rock cakes).

The first time I found something close after Granny and her stodge expertise passed on to the next realm was in Morocco, next to a mint tea. *Ghriba* are crackly-topped cookies often made with sesame seeds or ground almonds. They can be chewy inside, but I found a recipe that took me close to the simple, crumbly excellence of Granny's *kichels* on the blog *Cooking with Alia*. The recipe below is still close to Alia's, but now I brown the butter.

Throughout this chapter, I've been avoiding talking about 'washing down' a snack with your coffee because the imagery is so claggy, but I'm afraid it's unavoidable. The point of making the crumbliest biscuit in the world is exactly that you swish it down with your coffee. These little beige lumps are such good beacons for this book – they're nothing; they're just a bit of something; they're everything.

Makes about 22

115g unsalted butter
35g sesame seeds
285g plain flour
60g golden caster sugar
a pinch of fine sea salt
60ml vegetable oil

1. Preheat the oven to 180°C/160°C fan/gas 4, and line two baking trays.

2. Brown the butter: cut it into cubes and put it into a wide, shallow pan set over a medium heat. Watch it melt, picking up the pan and swirling intermittently to help the butter along. When it's all melted, it'll start to foam. Stick with it. Keep picking up the pan, swirling the butter, and taking a look. When you see brown flecks moving through the butter, you're done. It'll smell hazelnutty and toasty.

3. Transfer the brown butter to a small jug or bowl and leave it to cool.

4. Toast the sesame seeds in the buttery pan over a medium heat until golden.

5. In a mixing bowl, combine the flour, sugar, toasted sesame seeds and salt. Whisk or fork them together.

6. Add the oil and the melted butter to the dry ingredients, and mix them together with a knife until you have damp sand.

7. Then, form imperfect balls of dough in your hand – they should weigh about 20–25g apiece.

8. Arrange the balls on your lined baking trays, flattening them just a little with the back of a fork.

9. Bake the biscuits for 22–24 minutes – until they're light golden brown at the edges.

10. Leave to cool completely.

11. Get a plate.

This must be where pies go when they die

I had enjoyed coffee for a long time before I saw Agent Dale Cooper enjoying coffee in *Twin Peaks*, but I'm sure I must've started to enjoy it more afterwards. Agent Cooper's passion for coffee was so true, so infectious and so viscerally performed. Another first sip of coffee, 'black as midnight on a moonless night', and as Agent Cooper's head fug cleared before our eyes – the coffee appearing to do the job of an in-brain windscreen wiper – we were rooted back in the episode, even while the plot swilled into (delicious) idea soup. I could write thousands of words about the first coffee of the day but I will never make you look forward to tomorrow the way Kyle MacLachlan's face can.

At the Double R Diner, Norma (the diner's owner) arrives with Cooper's pie (huckleberry, this time) and he delivers the line you can now find on phone cases, mugs, pie plates and soy candles all over Etsy: *This must be where pies go when they die*. He's saying the pie is heavenly, so why was my first thought of a grizzly pie graveyard, decaying stone fruit as far as the eye can see, horrifying poorly latticed headstones? Either way, what's happening in this scene is that the pie is stopping Cooper in his tracks. He's taking a beat from his hushed and loopy conversation with Sheriff Truman, Big Ed Hurley, and Deputy Hawk. He gets right back to it afterwards: 'Someone's bringing drugs into Twin Peaks. Laura Palmer was on drugs. You call on Ed to help you out. Ed's a good man . . .'

This is coffee as an anchor. Coffee washing through your brain when nothing else can reach you. Coffee The Drink jolting you awake with stimulants, and Coffee The Experience swooping in like an arcade grabber and depositing you back in the middle of your life again. And pie is coffee's most precise food equivalent – the most articulate edible expression of cosiness, homeliness and comfort. For me, just the thought of pie helps, which is why I have so many pie cookbooks, despite finding the reality of regular pastry wrangling largely unrelaxing. But the books. The cosy, sturdy, steamy, constant loveliness of the books.

In *When Pies Fly*, Cathy Barrow sits me down and talks me through empanadas, strudels, stromboli, knishes and kolaches. She casually suggests that for your next Sunday brunch, you shape a tart like a bagel, fill it with herby cream cheese and top it with smoked salmon. There are 75 recipes in this book but it feels like a whole world. Bumbleberry Galette, PBJ Pie Poppers, Bet-You-a-Blueberry Frosted Hand Pies – are the names alone not poems?

And in *The Four & Twenty Blackbirds Pie Book* by Emily Elsen and Melissa Elsen, I get as swept up in glossy stories of aspirationally functional matrilineal love (the sister authors grew up in South Dakota eating, hanging out and eventually working in a restaurant run by their mum and aunties) as I do the six pages dedicated to tools like cherry pitters, mechanical apple peelers and marble slabs. Properly prepare your kitchen, the books seem to say, and you will ascend to pie paradise, which happens to have the exact same coordinates as general-purpose paradise. And even though I'm the kind of person who assumes festering stone fruit graveyards (or maybe because I am), I do want to order the OXO pastry blender the Elsens swear by.

Inspired by Agent Dale Cooper's beloved coffee snack and every word I have ever eaten about pie, I wrote the recipe below. It's a cherry pie in a Pop Tartish single serving (with marzipan), so that you can make a big batch and freeze it, thereby ascending to paradise on the regular simply by reading the instructions for baking from frozen at the bottom of the recipe. A sweet, buttery pie will be there for you, ready to oblige, next time you have a complex, multi-layered mystery to (pretend to) crack.

Cherry and marzipan hand pies

Makes 12–14

For the pastry
300g plain flour
a pinch of fine sea salt

2 tablespoons caster sugar
220g unsalted butter (or any vegan block-style butter), cold
150ml very cold water in a small bowl with 1 tablespoon
cider vinegar and 3 or 4 ice cubes

For the filling
300g frozen cherries
1 tablespoon lemon juice
60g caster sugar
1 tablespoon cornflour
a pinch of salt
50g golden marzipan
milk (any kind, for sealing)

1. Make the pastry at least 2 hours before you need it, or –
    even better – the night before.

2. Weigh the flour, salt and sugar into a bowl. Add the cold
    butter, cut into cubes.

3. Rub it all together between the tips of your (cold!) fin-
    gers until you have coarse crumbs.

4. Now begin to add the water-vinegar mix a tentative
    tablespoon at a time and mix it together gently with
    your hands. Just be mindful of handling the pastry as
    little as you can get away with.

5. When the dough is almost coming together, coax it into
    a ball. Then squish it slightly to a disc before wrapping
    it and putting it in the fridge.

6. Make the filling in advance, too. It should be completely cool when it hits the pastry. Put the cherries, lemon juice, sugar, cornflour and salt into a wide frying pan (off the heat) and stir until you can't see patches of white any more.

7. Turn the heat to low and keep the cherries moving while they release their juices. Squish them a bit with the back of your spoon.

8. Turn the heat up and bring to the boil. Let it bubble for a minute or two, until the liquid has thickened and stickified. Turn the heat off and leave to cool.

9. When you're ready to make the pies, take out the dough and give it 30 minutes to wake up before you attempt to roll it.

10. Meanwhile, preheat the oven to 190°C/170°C fan/gas 5 and line two baking trays. On a floured worktop, roll the pastry out to about 3mm thickness and cut it into circles with a 9–10cm cutter. Roll any scraps and repeat until it's all used up.

11. If at any point now, or over the next few instructions, the pastry feels warm and soft, give it a breather on a baking sheet in the fridge.

12. In half the circles, cut air vents – either make three slits with a sharp knife or take a very small cutter (2cm-ish) and cut a hole.

13. Now, time to fill. Have on standby: your cherry filling, your marzipan, a tiny cup of milk.

14. Arrange the non-vented circles across your baking trays and place about ½ tablespoon of cherries in the middle of each one.

15. Break tiny balls of marzipan from the block and dot them over the cherries.

16. Use a finger to run milk round the edges of the circle. Then take a vented circle, drape it over the top and press round the edges with a fork to crimp and seal.

17. Repeat with the remaining pastry and cherries, giving the formed pies ad hoc fridge breaks if they're a bit floppy.

18. Bake for about 20–24 minutes, or until they're deeply golden brown and erupting stickily through their air vents.

19. You can warm them up the next day in the toaster, Pop Tart-style.

To freeze, unbaked: place them on a baking tray in the freezer for a couple of hours. Then you can move them to a freezer bag and they won't stick together. Baking times won't be radically different – just a couple of minutes longer than you'd usually give them, but colour is your best guide.

Five pies of LA

1)

Du-pars is where you want to settle in and eat pie, with its brown leather, black and white tiles, and light that's gold like pastry. But I'm in a hurry so, regrettably, it's coconut pie to go or no coconut pie at all. Du-pars asks me, impatiently: 'Coconut cream or coconut custard?'

'What's the difference?' (I want the good one.)
'One has cream; one has custard.'

I spend the hot, hot day protecting my slice from becoming as oozy as I am. By the time I take it from its white box and eat it, the custard is lukewarm but supple, creamy and loaded with toasted desiccated coconut. I think I got the good one.

2)

We're on one of those drives that LA haters love to bang on about. It's painful, and we've heard Hotline Bling six times in the last hour, so we swerve off at Apple Pan. The horseshoe-shaped bar contains a man in a white paper hat, striding from customer to burger to pie slice.

The steakburger comes with a cinnamony relish in a greaseproof parcel that is made for your hand and mine – was made for our hands before we existed. My neighbour's coffee comes and makes him feel chatty. He's been coming here for 64 years. 'I share with my wife. She always gets the

[151]

pecan. She likes the pecan.' He then tells me, s l o w l y and
d e l i b e r a t e l y what the other flavours are –

banana cream
chocolate cream
boysenberry cream
apple.

He likes banana cream but has been getting pecan for 64
years because of love. Which is adorable, but of course I
have to get boysenberry cream because of magic (I'm from
the London Borough of Harrow; boysenberry might as well
be fairy dust).

3)

We are driving around looking for a cup of coffee and
I hear myself say: 'You're turning right on Sunset.' Is there a
more delicious thing you could ask your driver (husband) to
do? I turn it over in my mouth (you're turning right on
sunset) while watching the flash of palms in my window.

Four 'n' Twenty is an old restaurant with Tiffany lamps, vintage pie posters and small plastic pots of creamer. Our
waiter tells us the special pie is banana fudge with peanut
butter, like that's nothing.

There are slices of banana lost in the thickest, heaviest
blanket of custard, and there are whipped cream frills just
about everywhere. We wipe it out, and sit drinking coffee
in a daze. In some ways, my head is still there (and the
cream is probably still in my blood).

4)

The cherry pie at the 101 Coffee Shop wasn't a special or a seasonal pie. It was an ever-present pie, just as the 101 Coffee Shop was an ever-present diner, the kind of place you might go for Thanksgiving dinner and not be depressed. It had been the 101 Coffee Shop for 20 years when the pandemic shut it down. But it had also been a diner of some kind for decades before, and is now a diner of another kind. We move and we hope.

The 101 Coffee Shop cherry pie had loose, gloopy, bright red filling from a can and a shortcrust pastry case featuring no attempt at panache – no crimping, no latticing, no egg-washed elements. It wasn't about the pie, although of course it was, although you and I both know it wasn't.

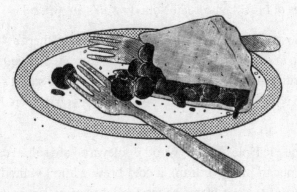

We'd decided to go to LA for a few months because we could. We'd bought a house in London that was being made habitable and some of our friends were pregnant. So we went to LA on a wave of panic and another stronger, sparklier wave of good ideas. There was a sense our time together in this way was ending – our time as young people (although no one could deny that we had strung out the concept of youth to the edges of plausibility).

One slice of pie, two forks. And long enough spent talking, panicking and laughing at the bar to need two top-ups from the coffee jug, which is (duh) what it's all about. You knew that.

5)

The Pie Hole on Hollywood Boulevard was 15 minutes' walk from where we were staying and no one walks in Hollywood, is what people repeat when they get home to show they've really got the measure of a place they haven't even tried to measure. Huge portions of pancakes! Many types of breakfast cereal! Nobody walks *anywhere*!

Opposite the Pie Hole is a parking lot and then there's a nail salon and then there's a smoothie bar, Deja Vu Showgirls, a burrito place. And, you know, as those people say, it's not even NICE, and once you've seen one star you've seen them all.

At the Pie Hole on Hollywood Boulevard I ate salted caramel pecan pie and drank a cold brew while I waited for Rich to get back from Trader Joe's. But maybe a parking lot on Hollywood Boulevard is the kind of thing you have to believe in to really see. Because as I sat, someone cordoned off the parking lot and it filled with the flashy, fluffy, shouty, red and black, behind-the-scenes hubbub of a real-life movie premiere. When Rich arrived, he got a pie slice of his own (because my slice was correctly portioned for one) and we craned our necks, and we watched.

When you're human garbage

Fika is sitting in a beautiful chair with a sheepskin on a cold but clear winter's day eating a cinnamon bun, and donuts are a special sugary trash reserved for when you're human garbage. To do fika you are probably beautiful with perfect hair and to do donut you are probably garbage. In this way and in more similar ways than we can count, we are robbed of joy.

The word fika is a flip of the two syllables in 'kaffe', it's a twice daily occurrence and employees at lots of Swedish companies fika mandatorily (it's a verb as well as a noun! Read the sentence again if you need to!). I suppose the difference is that in the UK or the USA we might be more compelled to donut al desko, and so we might not take the time (certainly not twice a day) to really notice our donuts.

In *The Donut Book*, Sally Levitt Steinberg writes:

'People disparage the donut, take it for granted without looking. Donuts are common, maybe, but a common favorite. Besides, how can something that is the lowest common denominator be unimportant? People eat donuts in a shop; a girl places them on a tray. Does the girl or the cop or the nurse stop to look, to ask why people love this thing, joke about it? Why does the donut invite, tickle, please, suggest? What is this ring I'm ruining by biting? Why does a monk meditate on it? The donut we have in hand we take for granted, until one day we notice. Noticing is what we are here for.'

And this book of mine is essentially 232 pages of noticing.

Now, do you like cake donuts or yeast donuts? If you spend a lot of time online, where you must regularly rank your biscuits and choose sides in debates about scones, you might think you're only allowed to love one donut type, or that you should like one donut type more than the other. Maybe you do, maybe you don't. My view, for what it's worth: joy is joy. Let's stop ranking everything.

To give you the facts: cake donuts are made of cake batter and yeast or 'raised' donuts are made of enriched bread dough – both are fried, unless 'baked' is specified in the title. Whether you think you love cake donuts or you suspect you're a yeasty person, I urge you to try the passionfruit and raspberry donuts that follow. They're crisp and juicy on the outside and soft and fluffy on the inside. They're perfect. Clearly, I'm not in the business of ranking my own recipes, but if I was, this might be my favourite. I wore a grin for days after I cracked these. I know! I buried the lede in the garbage. It's amazing what you can find down here.

Passionfruit and raspberry cake donuts

NOTE: I'm sorry; you need quite a few non-negotiable things: round cutters (or donut cutters), a spider strainer, a thermometer, kitchen paper, a wire rack.

Makes about 8 donuts and 16 donut holes

175g plain flour
1¼ teaspoons baking powder
¼ teaspoon salt
75g golden caster sugar
120g sour cream
1 egg
1 teaspoon vanilla extract
15g unsalted butter, melted and cooled
65g raspberries
rapeseed oil, for frying (about 1.5 litres)

For the glaze
2 large passionfruits (or 3–4 small ones)
200g icing sugar
1–2 tablespoons milk

1. Make the glaze first; just get this cute little job done. Stir the seeds and juice from the passionfruits into the icing sugar and add milk a little at a time until you have a thin gloop. Passionfruits unhelpfully yield varying amounts of juice, but the main thing to know is that the glaze must be thick enough to envelop the donuts, but not thick enough that you could call it icing.

2. In a mixing bowl, whisk together the flour, baking powder, salt and sugar.

3. In a jug or small bowl, whisk together the sour cream, egg, vanilla and melted butter until smooth and even.

4. Add half the wet ingredients to the dry ingredients and mix with a spatula until only just combined. Repeat with the other half, but just *before* everything is combined, add the raspberries. Break them up as you add them to the bowl and work them very gently into the batter until there are no floury pockets. Interfere as little as you can while still getting the job done.

5. Leave the batter in its bowl and place it in the fridge for 10 minutes.

6. Now get your station sorted. Clear up (I'm not a clean-as-I-go person at all but it really has to be done here) and liberally flour your worktop.

7. Pour the oil into a deep saucepan so that it comes 5–8cm up the sides. Start heating it gently with the thermometer in it, bearing in mind you're aiming for 180°C to fry.

8. Arrange several sheets of kitchen paper next to the fryer.

9. Take your batter out of the fridge and pat it to about 2cm thickness on your floured worktop. It'll be really sticky and tricky to handle, so use lots of flour – don't hold back.

10. Cut the donuts out, keeping their holes; I use an 8cm cutter for the donut and a 2.5cm cutter for the hole. Repat and cut more from the scraps. The less you handle the dough the better, though, so if it comes to it, go for more holes and fewer rings.

11. When the oil hits 180°C, fry 3 donuts at a time, prodding and turning them with your spider strainer, until they're golden brown all over.

12. Move them to the kitchen-paper zone.

13. When the donuts are warm, not hot, place a wire rack over a plate or baking sheet to catch any glaze run-off. Stir the glaze. Dunk the donuts in the glaze and give them a good wiggle around, flipping them over and making sure they're covered all over.

14. Transfer them to the wire rack.

15. When the glaze has firmed up, and not a second later: eat.

A GLASS OF WINE

I don't know what I'm talking about (but why should that stop me?)

I get overfaced by pub wine measures. I know that doesn't make me sound very young and hip and cool but I really don't know how to handle a gravy boat of Merlot. I mean this literally: I don't know how to hold it. On the X axis, the wine is getting warmer and on the Y axis I am enjoying it less and on some other axis buzzing away while I try to have a chat, there is a jagged zigzag of panic and acid reflux. It's not about the quantity of wine overall, but the ruthless functionality of the pour, the brash boatiness of the glass. No more, no less than 125ml, or 175ml, or 250ml. Take it away and do not come back here, clogging up the bar, standing on tippy-toe trying to get served.

It's also to do with the lack of snacks. I am an eating person at heart; that means I much prefer to be eating than not eating, and so I need more than one little bag of crisps between four, torn open to expose the seven to eight crisps within. That will not see me through 175ml of Merlot. But, you know, maybe I don't want Cumberland sausages either! Or Thai fish cakes! Maybe I don't want a Scotch egg the size of a basketball, thank you so much! I'm looking for something that will help set the pace for me, reassure my brain that I don't need to knock this jumbo acid bomb back like an

EastEnder who just received news of a terrible affair. I need a few plates arriving at the table at different times. I need it all to be significantly less stringent, less large, more delicious, more . . . European.

I like the pub. I am grateful for her quizzes, her friendship, her Sundays, her fires, her last orders, her garden, her moody maroons. But I *love* aperitivo hour in almost any European city, where the wine sloshes in at 2 euros a glass and the snacks are thoughtful rewards for making it through the day. Careful salty parcels that might be cheesy, zingy, or crunchy; deep-fried, pickled, or grilled; made with pig's heads, anchovies or olives.

And crisps, yes. Always crisps. But as many as you can eat, not 40g, cordially divided.

Don't think this snobbery means I am any kind of an expert in drinking wine. I have tried. We have taken to curating a Library of Loved Wines above our kitchen cabinets. If we've enjoyed a bottle, we rinse it out and stick it up there. It's not what I would call a system, because the moment one of us sets a bottle atop our kitchen's head, any details we were able to glean about the wine instantly erase themselves from our deadened 2022 minds.

I have tried to get serious. I've filled notepads and I've bought all the fat books – the bibles and the atlases. I went through a phase of drinking only wines from Beaujolais so that I could get friendly with the Gamay grape, and learn to discern between the personalities of Beaujolais' little mini-regions (Beaujolais *crus*). I gave up when I heard a sommelier say this was a bad place to start because 'there's not a huge amount of variety from Beauj to Beauj'.

There are so many factors that go into knowing wine 'properly' – pure memory (learning the regions, the grapes, the vineyards and the winemakers), a well-trained nose (you need to know what a geranium leaf smells like and be able to call it up instantly), barrels and barrels of spare time and cash. But the thing that intimidates me the most is the self-belief you're supposed to summon to taste in other people's company. Before you announce what you've sniffed out, you must absolutely believe it, or at least be willing to say it as though you do. And if it turns out you're wrong (strawberry, not cherry, you dunderhead), you need to be able to shrug it off.

But I am a chronically embarrassed person. I'm embarrassed now, as I write about my embarrassment. I get embarrassed: playing crazy golf, asking for Canesten Once at the pharmacy, pronouncing pain au chocolat, when you tell me there's parsley in my teeth, parking the car, when I can't hear you very well, when you ask me what my book is about. I want to learn more about wine because I'm sick of living an embarrassed life. 'Lychee!' I will pronounce, and you will tell me it's melon, and I won't care. That's my fantasy.

There's one thing I know: you can't separate the wine from the experience – and I'm not currently committed enough to the cause to try. I won't be forgoing toothpaste or coffee to get the best sense of a bottle of wine. What I will do (because it's my favourite thing to do in the world) is sit at a table with a friend and plough through crackers smushed with mushroom pâté, or mayonnaise spooned on halved boiled eggs while our (scantily filled) glasses empty without us noticing. Should you wish to do that in your own home, this chapter is full of snacks that will make whatever wine you're drinking taste like the sun. Write it in your notepad. *This one tastes like the fucking sun*. It's true if you believe it.

A snack on a stick

In Rioja I encountered *gilda* in huge numbers, piled high on silver platters at bars where glasses of rosado cost £1.50. *Gilda* is a classic lil' *pintxo* on a cocktail stick (*pintxo* is Basque for *pincho*, which is Spanish for *spike*) made up of olives, anchovies and pickled chillies. And it took me a few days to give *gilda* a go because I was taken in by bigger, floozier *pintxos* containing garlic mushrooms, ham and hot potatoes.

But once I started on those spikes, I didn't stop. A *gilda* is spicy, salty and acidic all at once – a frenzy of flavour. To pop a pile of them next to you at home when the clock strikes aperitivo is to turn a moment into an event. Play with the ingredients to find your combo – add a pickled silverskin onion if you like, go nuts.

You'll need wine with oomph – something that's game for a flavour skirmish. Just like you. Plus:

Fat, green olives without stones
Pickled guindilla chillies in a jar
Anchovy fillets in olive oil
Cocktail sticks

Thread all three items on to your stick, folding the chilli and anchovy in half. It's . . . food sewing?

Over-whipped cream

I'm not the kind of Snack Author™ that would try to pull the wool over your eyes and so now feels like the time to admit: there's no finer snack to eat with a glass of wine than a chunk of fresh bread spread thickly with salty butter.

We appear to be living through the dough years (and the d'oh years). The world is a flaming, convulsing bin, so we're trying to bake ourselves better. Restaurant bread baskets are trying, too. Now, you might find yourself eating slices from three different loaves (a loaf flight, if you will) before your dinner arrives – a focaccia, a soda, a sour. A disc of house salted butter on the side. This is so often the best bit, the moment you congratulate yourself for your choices.

It has been consistently proven in clinical trials (done by me) that having a block of house salted butter on hand improves overall effectiveness (of you) by tonnes of per cent. And I don't know about you but for a minute there I forgot something I learned when I was six at the dairy farm on Kenton Lane: that butter is churned cream. If you want something more heavenly and exhilarating than you can possibly imagine (do you? I bet you do), the 'recipe' below takes, I kid you not, 10 minutes.

May your snacks be salty and silky, whatever happens next.

Salted butter

300ml double cream
5g fine sea salt OR 4g fine sea salt and 2g flaky sea salt, if
    you like salty surprises

(if you don't trust the accuracy of your scales, add the salt a half or a quarter teaspoon at a time and taste as you go – as below.)

1. Pour the double cream into a large bowl and use an electric mixer on medium speed to whisk it to soft peaks, then stiff peaks, and beyond . . .

2. It'll start to separate – the butter will clump up in the beaters and the buttermilk will slosh around the bowl. When you have two distinct products, use a sieve to

separate them entirely. Squeeze the butter in your hands to get as much buttermilk out as possible. You can use the buttermilk to make cake, soda bread, or a smoothie.

3. Put some cold water and a few ice cubes into a clean bowl. Rinse the butter here, squeezing it to release any lingering buttermilk. Repeat with a second bowl of iced water.

4. Put your butter on a piece of greaseproof paper and pat it out to a rough rectangle, about a centimetre thick. Sprinkle over the fine sea salt and knead it in – add it gradually if you prefer, and taste as you go. If you like the crunch of salt flakes, add and knead this in too.

5. Pat the butter into a cute circle, wrap it up in greaseproof paper, and refrigerate. It'll keep for up to a week.

I'm not a regular tin of fish, I'm a cool tin of fish

Making mum friends is hard and my technique is probably the worst of all. What I do is I meet them and then I hope. I hope that I've gleaned enough details to track them down on Instagram (I usually have, I'm essentially an interrogator) or I hope that I'll see them again at the park. I made one friend via Borrow My Doggy (she is so nice she will probably be the first to read this book – hello, Rosie). Her adorable family started borrowing my doggy, basically.

A few months into our fledgling friendship, Rosie was in Lisbon, and my mind and mouth being the way they are, I started waffling about tinned fish. She hadn't expressed any interest in tinned fish at all, but there I was, prodding her towards the Conserveira de Lisboa, essentially a (stunning!) tinned fish museum, when she just wanted to make sandcastles, drink sangria and enjoy her life. As the chat splintered to a close, I remembered that not everyone knows or cares about tinned fish, the kind that comes festooned with art and served in wine bars. Not everyone has noticed that the snobbiest eaters in the UK and the USA have recently declared it 'cool', though the people of Spain and Portugal have been conserving this way for well over a century. And even if people do know or care about this, they may not themselves be interested in seeking out tinned fish on holiday, because they associate it with olden times, or pets, or just because they have better things to do.

I let it go, because if I had tried to explain myself, things would've got weirder. And that's just to say that if you're a young person trying to make friends: it doesn't necessarily get easier. But I don't lose sleep about making things weird any more – I just write about it.

Personally, I will happily eat tinned sardines on toast with zero mod cons, but in my household, only our matchmaking dog Peggy would do the same. On a night in on my own, with nobody to make things weird for, I would consider sardines, toast and an old lump of lemon a perfect dinner. But some people need more convincing than I do. And even if you love tinned sardines, you still might not think of them as a snack capable of sitting prettily on a gingham tablecloth at a Thing. But if this book is here to teach you anything at all, it's that the difference between a snack you eat alone and a snack you serve to others is just a bit of delicious flimflam.

To win over the sardine sceptics, you must begin by invoking the Med with a thick, deeply yellow, garlicky-as-all-hell aïoli. Then you must make a nod to oyster bars with a bowl of tinily chopped mignonette-ish onion and parsley. Finally, you need the flourish that only a hard-boiled egg can bring, chopped to a sprinkle. You're creating a sort-of sardine bar here. Put all these bits and bobs into your cutest bowls, and watch the fishy philistines lap it up, like cats (Rosie? Are you on your way?).

A sardine party

Serves 4

2 eggs
1 brown onion, finely chopped
3 tablespoons chopped parsley
juice of 1 lemon
1 batch of aïoli (page 223)
lots of toast
2 tins of sardines in oil
flaky salt
Aleppo chilli flakes
black pepper

NOTE: When making the aïoli you can replace the extra virgin olive oil with oil from the sardine tin, if you find it to be delicious enough.

1. Set 2 eggs boiling. You want them hard all the way through – no squidge (11 minutes on a rolling boil, or whatever alternative method you favour).

2. When the eggs are done, cool them off under the tap, peel them and chop them into tiny pieces. Put the pieces into a cute little bowl.

3. Combine the onion, parsley and lemon juice in another cute little bowl and toss well with a fork.

4. Make your aïoli if you haven't already.

5. Everyone at the table should assemble their toast as they see fit but I would do this: i) thick schmear of aïoli; ii) sardines straight from the tin, mashed with a fork; iii) sprinkle of onion and parsley; iv) sprinkle of egg; v) flaky salt, chilli flakes, black pepper.

One more tin: tuna with roasted red peppers

The best snacks take hold of your evening when you don't worry too much about what they are. Is it an open sandwich? A small plate? A bit of something? A tin of fish tipped on to a dish? I ate a tuna thing like this at a wine tasting in Rioja. Before the winemakers opened their bottles and their hearts to us, we chatted across a language barrier and a table that appeared to be expecting many more guests. There it was, among the riches: tinned tuna, roasted red peppers and the winemakers' own olive oil. Truly beautiful to behold, a perfect, no-nonsense bit of something to accidentally slosh a little wine over. To be honest, it's not much of anything at all without a lot of bread to smush it up from the plate and into your mouth, but few things are.

Serves 2

1 red pepper (or jarred red pepper)
3 tablespoons extra virgin olive oil
1 tablespoon sherry vinegar
1 x 150g (ish) tin of tuna in brine
black pepper
bread, to serve

NOTE: I suggest using tuna packed in brine, because this way it's easier to drain the tuna and have full control over how it's dressed. If you have tuna in olive oil, by all means use the oil from the tin if it tastes good to you. If you have tuna in not-tasty oil, just drain it as best you can.

1. If you're using a jarred red pepper, proceed to step 3 and ignore step 5. If you're using a fresh pepper, rest it directly over a naked flame on a gas hob and turn it occasionally to blacken and crackle the skin all over. (Roast it in the oven if you don't have a gas hob.)

2. Put your freshly charred pepper into a Tupperware with the lid on or a sealed freezer bag while you get the other bits ready.

3. Measure the oil and vinegar straight on to a dinner plate and swirl into a pinkish slick.

4. Use a fork to arrange the drained tuna over the plate.

5. Over the sink, rub the rested, charred pepper between your fingers to remove the blistered skin. Then deseed it.

6. Chop the pepper into thin strips, and drape them over the tuna.

7. Finish with a few twists of black pepper and serve, with bread.

Why does Paris make me want to eat a pig's head?

Was there a time that Paris seemed *less* exciting than other places because of its geographical proximity to my humdrum life? I think there might've been. It was a place you could go on a school trip. You spent your parents' money on tat at the bottom of the Eiffel Tower – balloons filled with flour with smiley faces on them that were destined to explode catastrophically on the coach – and you walked down the Champs-Élysées, aware (despite being 12) that you wouldn't really want to go to London and walk down Oxford Street. And your teachers pointed out how people here didn't care that much about zebra crossings and you noticed that people here really did care about baguettes. And the way people spoke their whirling, velvet language made you quite sure you'd never get the hang of it, but nonetheless you waited your turn to go into the shop and ask for *un* (not *une*) *timbre, s'il vous plaît* for your *carte postale*, which would reach your own home long after you had.

But then doesn't it turn out that one of the UK's greatest gifts is (urgh, was) its relationship with Europe and its proximity to Paris? And travelling doesn't just mean putting a back-pack on your back and staying in a faraway hostel with a rat problem. It means everything: the coach, the stamps, the flour balloons, the baguettes, the zebra crossings.

And what does it actually mean to immerse yourself in a culture? If you eat a late-night McDo are you doing it wrong? If you like the look of the boulanger's granary loaf, does your holiday still count? If you go to an ornate French cinema and watch *Ant-Man*, is that fine?

The thing about Paris is that it's so completely itself, so utterly poised, so bluntly sure of itself, you can't not immerse yourself, no matter what you do. You get off the train and a few minutes ago you were in Ebbsfleet and now you are here, in Paris, where Remy the rat made ratatouille and Carrie Bradshaw stayed in suite 609 of the Hôtel Plaza Athénée.

Paris, where the Tabac sells tobacco and metro tickets and lotto tickets and glass bottle Oranginas. There are shots of espresso in paper cups. You've got to buy a *carnet de billets* if you want to get on the Metro, and the stations are called Rambuteau and Opéra and Chemin Vert and everyone is on a lunchbreak.

If it's a bit early for a drink but you want one anyway, you can just get a demi-pêche (a small beer with peach syrup in it) at a pavement table. Later, on the same pavement, or a different one, whether you're celebrating anything specific or not, you can get a kir royale (a glass of champagne with crème de cassis in it). Some shops are open, some are closed, the shopkeepers decide their own fates. And there are chicken rôtisseries on street corners with sliced potatoes underneath, glistening.

You might not even see the Eiffel Tower, or it might spring into the sky when you're least expecting it. The air is cosy and rich and sparkling with the Paris of it all. You may well be dining on the other Royale and a red sleeve of *frites*, but you are in Paris.

Here we are, then. I am plonking my bags on the parquet flooring of my Airbnb and tidying up my smudged eyeliner so I can get straight out there and eat a pig's head. That's just how it is. I'm off to sit down with a glass of wine and a small plate of terrine de campagne, which isn't even fancy, by the way. Terrines and pâtés are just regular here. They're the food of the people. I am not necessarily more immersed than you are, but I sure am here.

Pork rillettes

Obviously, I had never made rillettes at home before I started researching this book. It's just not a thing for regular people to do in a private home. I might've considered eating rillettes at home if I'd overdone it at the deli counter, or performed a supermarket sweep at the Eurostar terminal, but not just as a matter of course. Not on a weekday and not on a weekend either.

Rillettes date back to the 15th century; they are not pâté and they're not terrine; they're a more casual porky smush, with enough fat to do the job of butter on hot toast. The pork is slow-cooked in its own fat (confit) with lots of lovely gentle spice (I settled on woodsy juniper and warm, wintry all-spice). As far as at-home charcuterie goes, rillettes are the easiest. An out-there and brilliant book I have called *French Regional Cooking* by Anne Willan says rillettes are 'simplicity itself to make' – I mean, you just cook the meat slowly until it falls apart. It's embarrassing to admit I thought you had to be in a wine bar to eat them.

My research told me you're meant to use back fat, but my local butcher told me three times she didn't have any back fat (because she'd used it all up in her sausages), and that was enough for me to decide against instructing you all to find back fat. I made my rillettes happen with pork belly alone and I loved it. I think you need more fat if you want to keep your rillettes in the fridge for several months. But this is a merry little snack book, not a charcuterie manual (to that end I recommend Jane Grigson's *Charcuterie and French Pork Cookery*), and I'm not the woman to recommend you keep anything in the fridge for several months without eating it. This is a cosy, comfy, confit snack that – with the help of cornichons – makes for a late-night power plate best set on a soft sofa blanket when everyone else has gone to bed. Not in three months, but tonight.

Serves 6

1.2kg pork belly, rind and bones removed (about 800–900g once trimmed)
5 cloves of garlic, crushed or minced

8 juniper berries, crushed
3 bay leaves
4 sprigs of thyme
125ml dry white wine
100ml water
fine sea salt
black pepper
ground allspice

1. Preheat the oven to 140°C/120°C fan/gas 1.

2. Cut the pork belly into 2.5cm cubes.

3. Put the pork into a large casserole with the crushed garlic, crushed juniper, bay leaves, thyme, wine, water, one teaspoon of fine sea salt and a few twists of black pepper.

4. Set the pan over a medium heat until the liquid just bubbles. Then put the lid on and leave it in the oven for 4 hours, checking and stirring halfway through.

5. Set up a sieve over a large mixing bowl and tip the pork and all its fats and juices into the sieve.

6. Press the pork into the sieve with the back of a spoon, mix and repeat, until you've coaxed everything juicy into the bowl. The idea is to squeeze liquid fat out of any visible chunks of fat and to discard any bits of gristle you don't fancy meeting later.

7. Move the pork to another bowl, pick out the thyme branches (everything else will have dissolved), and pull the meat to shreds using two forks (or you can use the

paddle attachment of an electric mixer). Gradually add back enough of the liquid fat to make it creamy and delicious (usually all of it, for me).

8. Season: add more salt if you need to. Add ground allspice a tentative pinch at a time, plus more ground black pepper to taste.

9. Leave to cool, then refrigerate and eat within a week. Serve with cornichons and hot toast.

Mushroom pâté

And because we all know that we should be eating much less pig's head, here's how to take a punnet of mushrooms to primo, A1, peak physical shroominess, prime for piling on to a cracker.

Serves 6

30g walnuts
30–40g dried porcini mushrooms
2 tablespoons olive oil
1 shallot, roughly chopped
1 clove of garlic, crushed or minced
340g fresh chestnut, shiitake or portobello mushrooms, peeled and roughly chopped
salt and pepper
40ml Madeira
2 tablespoons crème fraîche (or any vegan alternative)
1 tablespoon light soy sauce
1 tablespoon roughly chopped tarragon

1. Toast the walnuts in a dry frying pan, shimmying them occasionally, until slightly darkened and smelling nutty.

2. In a small bowl, hydrate the dried mushrooms using 300ml of boiling water.

3. Heat the 2 tablespoons of olive oil in a medium frying pan and when it's hot, add the shallot. Cook gently for at least 15 minutes, until really soft and starting to take on colour. Then add the garlic to the pan and cook for 2 more minutes.

4. Add all the fresh mushrooms to the pan with a small pinch of salt and toss well with the shallot and garlic. Once the mushrooms have got going and released lots of liquid, turn the heat up to help things along. Cook for about 10 minutes, until the liquid has evaporated.

5. Add the rehydrated mushrooms and their soaking water to the pan and cook until that's all gone, too.

6. Add the Madeira to the pan and cook until the pan is mostly dry (there should be no running liquid when you move your spoon across it).

7. Let the mushroom mix cool to lukewarm, then blitz it in a food processor with the crème fraîche, walnuts, soy sauce and tarragon. I like it quite coarse so you get the crunch of the walnuts, but you should take it as smooth as you like.

8. Season to taste.

Double eggs

For a time (I wish I could tell you what time, or for how long, or even roughly when), my daughter kept muttering about double eggs. We couldn't work it out, because it's not an expression we (or anyone?) uses and yet here she was, in her high chair, apparently demanding double eggs. Was it possible she wanted us to provide twice the eggs she was used to? She couldn't count yet, but could she . . . double? No. We eventually realised she was practising the alphabet and getting stuck, as we all have, on 'W, X'.

But now I think of her double eggs whenever I make mayonnaise for the express purpose of adding it to eggs. I like to make mayonnaise all the time, and I believe deeply in its power to boost a roast chicken, a sandwich, a potato salad and your life, but there is nothing I like to make mayonnaise for more than eggs themselves. You start with a yolk and a sprinkle of flaky salt and you end up spooning swathes of smooth mayonnaise on top of yet more eggs. W, X, Y and Z.

My birthday in 2020 was most people's last day in the office. The weekend after, we were supposed to be having friends over for the lunch of my dreams, but we had to cancel because I had a cough. We didn't have time to cancel the food shop, which was (unlike the very many online food shops to come) highly impractical: mostly eggs and Beaujolais. We made the lunch anyway, for ourselves; we ate oeufs dur mayonnaise as lavishly as we could, and it was sort of nice, but it was sort of breathtakingly ominous, in the way that things were if you knew you were one of the lucky ones, with a warm house, food to eat and company to drive crazy. We would get through the eggs, that wouldn't be a problem. But when would we be able to do this with other people again? When would my nan eat an egg with another person again?

Egg mayonnaise is magnificent in any format, but of course oeufs dur mayonnaise are my guys. They are boiled eggs halved with a big dollop of mayonnaise on them, and then a garnish of the cook's choice. To me, they are Parisian pavements in spring; they are a breakfast glass of Beauj; they are baskets and baskets of baguette. They are time and freedom and people and magical, magical Eurostars.

The way to do them with your friends and your wine if you have the luxuries of good health and freedom to share communal bowls is to set up an oeuf station. You halve the boiled eggs and arrange them with the yolks facing sunnily outward and you serve a bumper bowl of mayonnaise and plenty of bread to break. Then you provide a suite of serving suggestions – from the glamorous (caviar!) to the basic (hot sauce!). And if you want to send the people truly loopy, you just add crispy potato (that tip works for most scenarios).

The oeuf station

For 6 boiled eggs, use 1 batch (or 225g) of mayonnaise (page 222).

Cook the eggs however you like them. For this, I'd use the Delia method so the yolks still have a little squidge: place the eggs in a large saucepan with enough cold water to cover by 1cm. Bring the water to a boil, then swiftly turn it down to a simmer and set a timer for 6 minutes. Drain and cool under a running tap before peeling.

Garnishes

Finely chopped chives or spring onions

Chopped cornichons

Capers

Individual anchovies from a jar

Fish roe

Black sesame seeds

Smoked paprika

Hot sauce

Crispy fried shallots *(slice them as thinly as you can and then fry the tiny rings in 2–3cm of very hot vegetable oil. Cook, using a spider strainer to keep things moving, until all the moisture has disappeared and they start turning golden brown; lift them out with your strainer and let them drain on lots of kitchen paper. It happens very suddenly, so be on your guard.)*

The Côte d'Azur knows what it's doing

One holiday in Nice, my fondness for staring at palm fronds against blue skies while mindlessly munching snacks and drinking rosé led to Rich getting heatstroke. I'm not a good nurse (or person) so I didn't let that stop me. By the last night he was thoroughly unwell, unable to hold down the Coca-Colas I insisted would see him right.

A quick disclaimer then before we continue: enjoy snacks in the blazing sunshine at your own risk. Look after your loved ones.

As we've established, France knows exactly how to pepper a day of drinking with snacks – a slice of terrine here, a mayo-swirled egg there, a neat little trio of cheeses just as you start to get antsy. So, throw in a Côte d'Azur location and it's no surprise things can get a little dehydrated.

But if you're in it (and by it, I mean life) for the snacks, Nice is for you. There are wide boulevards lined with the vivid vegetables of your dreams: artichokes and aubergines to take back to your Airbnb for later. And then there are exquisitely holidayish, narrow, shady alleyways to wander: sun piercing through wherever it gets the chance, little wobbly tables with icy glasses of rosé on them and hot, fresh snacks galore. There is pissaladière, a rectangular flatbread topped with caramelised onions, anchovies and black olives (someone has laboured over onions until they're bronze and sweet, so you don't have to). There's ratatouille (someone has sautéd vegetables slice by slice so you can enjoy your holiday). And there are delicate fried courgette flowers (someone has literally stood over a vat of hot oil in the blazing heat so you can eat this flower of gold). And there is socca.

Soccas are crêpes made using chickpea flour, cooked until bronzed, blistered and crispy. Socca pros use giant, flat copper pans, which they slide into ferociously hot wood-fired ovens to meet the open flames. The socca is served in rough, jubilant shards, scraped straight from the hotplate. My version (to follow) is designed for your regular, hospitable home oven. But if the socca gets stuck, do as the pros do: scrape.

Socca

A healthy person can eat an unlimited quantity of socca. It's delicious as it is – a crispy, olive-oily, savoury snack – but it's even better if you have something to dip into (try the cashew, kale and Parmesan dip on page 59 or any garlicky tomato sauce), plus a scattering of black olives, and pints upon pints of delicious, crisp, cold tap water.

Makes 3 pancakes

175g gram flour
¾ teaspoon fine sea salt
black pepper
350ml lukewarm water
2 tablespoons olive oil
more olive oil

1. In a mixing bowl, whisk the flour, salt and several twists of black pepper to combine.

2. Make a little well in the middle and pour the water in gradually, whisking as you go and incorporating more flour along the way, until you have a smooth and very loose batter.

3. Whisk through the 2 tablespoons of olive oil.

4. Heat your oven to 240°C/220°C fan/gas 9. Coat the bottom of a 23cm cake tin with olive oil (about 2 tablespoons) and put the tin into the warming oven. Let the batter sit while you do this.

5. When the oven and tin are hot, ladle in enough batter to cover the bottom of the tin and bake in the oven for 16–20 minutes or until you have a pancake that's really golden brown and crispy. Repeat for each pancake.

6. Ease it from the tin with a spatula and cut it into pizza-style slices or shards to serve.

Not in favour of: pretending

Let's talk about bodge jobs. If a snack can be a Mini Cheddar or a gougère, we have to accept there's something in between. Your friend is coming for a drink and you want to *do something* but you don't want to, you know, *do something*. Your friend would be happy with Hula Hoops. My friends would be happy with a glass of water even if I ran it too warm, but look, I like them.

I learned about mince pie pinwheels when I had a four-month-old baby and Christmas was coming. Did I want you to feel that there was some semblance of Christmas cheer beneath my sallow face and soggy muslins? Yes. Did I have the time, wherewithal or mental capacity to actually promote that concept? No. I took some bog standard jarred mince-meat and a sheet of bog standard puff pastry and I rolled it up with all the devotion of someone enveloping a dead body in an old carpet. And what did you get when you walked through the front door? Warmth and love and cloves and pastry and Christmas. (Something to bear in mind: you can't always tell when your snack has been prepared with despair.)

Nonetheless, it's handy to know about pinwheels, and it would be remiss of me to write a snack book without unfurling any pre-made, ready-rolled puff pastry.

The two recipes that follow are about quickly packing a huge umami hit within layers of puff pastry. They are both completely ideal for urgent last-minute drink-and-rants at your kitchen table. They are *not* about concealing your chaotic inner life until a more 'convenient' moment presents itself. Please don't do that. Unfurl your emotional Jus-Rol – let it all hang loose.

Tapenade pinwheels

Makes 16

1 x 320g sheet of ready-rolled puff pastry
6 tablespoons (90g) tapenade or olive paste (see page 218 if you want to make your own)
115g crumbly goat's cheese (optional)

1. Preheat the oven to 200°C/180°C fan/gas 6.

2. Carefully unroll your sheet of puff pastry, keeping it on its sheet of baking paper, and place it so the long side is nearest you (landscape).

3. Spread the tapenade evenly over the pastry.

4. Break and crumble the goat's cheese over the top (if you're using it).

5. From the side nearest you, roll upwards like a Swiss roll, using the paper to guide you.

6. With a sharp knife, cut the log you've created into 16 slices (to help keep them evenly sized, cut in half, then quarters, then eighths, then sixteenths).

7. Place the 16 pinwheels swirl-side-up on a baking sheet and bake for 18–20 minutes, until the pastry is puffed up and golden.

Tomato and anchovy puffs

Makes 8

1 x 320g sheet of ready-rolled puff pastry
½ tablespoon olive oil
1 clove of garlic, crushed or minced
2 anchovies
150g tinned chopped tomatoes
30g Parmesan, finely grated
125g ball of mozzarella

1. Preheat the oven to 200°C/180°C fan/gas 6, and line two baking trays.

2. Carefully unroll your sheet of puff pastry (keeping it on its paper). Cut it in half, then divide each half into four even rectangles.

3. In a frying pan, heat the olive oil over a medium flame. When it's hot, add the garlic and anchovies. Smush the

anchovies with the back of your spoon and cook for a minute or two, until the anchovies and garlic are one with the oil.

4. Add the tomatoes, mashing any chunks with the back of your spoon, and cook for not very long at all, just until it's thickened up a little. Season to taste.

5. Split the pastry rectangles between the two baking trays.

6. Use a teaspoon to dollop tomato sauce in the middle of each rectangle, and sprinkle Parmesan on top.

7. Tear a few little chunks of mozzarella and place them on and around the tomato, too. It's all going to ooze outwards.

8. Take the top left-hand corner and the bottom right-hand corner and fold them inwards to meet over the filling, overlapping them by a couple of centimetres. Press together to seal (don't worry about neatness).

9. Bake for 22–25 minutes, until the pastry is puffed up and golden and the cheesy, saucy filling is bubbling.

SNACKS ON ICE

Sun slopping

In the summer of 2018, I was finishing *Carbs*. I was a muddle of 'final' thoughts on how things should look, taste and sound. My brain rushed all day and then thrashed all night. I'd wake up thinking, Gorgonzola. No, neon green. No, what about marjoram? The thoughts were never breakthroughs. My brain was in overdrive.

But this was the summer I learned to embrace tiny bits of time out. There was no holiday in my near future and I wasn't anticipating a weekend off, but I could grab 20 minutes here and there to slop about the local park in glittery slides and pick up a giant watermelon quarter on my way home. So I did! I slopped whenever I could. I sat on the grass and looked at the leaves on the trees and marvelled at how often the volunteers revived the flower beds. If I'd already slopped three times that day I didn't let that stop me going again.

I have a one-track mind so I rarely took time out without refreshments. I found the corner shop's Diet Cokes were a whole £1.50 cheaper than the ones for sale in the park, and while I was there I slid back their freezer doors to rummage for the fruitiest lollies in the frost. My trinity of summertime mindfulness: Diet Coke, watermelon, ice lolly.

Two summers later we would nickname the same park the 'prison yard'. We could do nothing but circle it, once a day, trying to avoid the many people who seemed not to care about this new thing called 'social distancing'. Though I couldn't find a jolt of joy in my surroundings, which just reinforced how stuck we all were, I could occasionally find it in a can of something fizzy. But this can was different from 2018's cans, because it had been painstakingly ordered in an eight-pack to save multiple trips to the shop. On the face of it, my daily outlet was the same (a walk in the park) but obviously – everyone knew – its essence was gone. The freedom had been the whole point of all that slopping. Now, any walk I took was as purposeful as eating breakfast, taken unsloppily at a point in the day that suited my family's specific and unwavering routine. When the time came, I strode carefully, more aware of the space I was inhabiting than I'd ever been.

I couldn't stop for watermelons, cans or lollies, and even if I did (because I also needed some essentials) I did so jacked up with the grim feeling that I shouldn't be – and the fear of what might be waiting invisibly on the freezer door. A person wouldn't be rummaging in there. A person would have to take whatever was on the top. This is what we might forget – that many of the things we could do sucked as hard as the things we couldn't.

You can never be too good at living moment to moment, can you? This whole book is about tiny, juicy moments of freedom and in the summer, things get juicier. And yes, it's true that many of the ways we snack in the summertime are liquid, but then again, some of them are salty, buttery corn on the cobs. Go grab them all while you can.

Saturday morning yoghurt drinks

Ever since I've been aware of the concept of Saturday morning, my dad has played badminton on it. When we were all younger, badminton Saturdays were a scene. Afterwards, he'd have a fry-up at our house or his friend Andrew's and they'd play a game of chess. On the way, he'd buy a bottle of raspberry Yop, as though there was simply no way of making it from badminton to breakfast without this yoghurty bridge.

We the children weren't really allowed Yop, so it rooted itself in my brain as a luxury item, like Alpen. These days, my favourite Turkish lunch spot in Hackney serves a perfect 'frappé' – an icy blend of strawberries, bananas, honey and yoghurt. And in LA, the nicest thing I ever drank is not a Tequila Sunrise or even a marg, but the orange blossom yoghurt drink at Kismet Falafel, attempted with utmost respect in the selection that follows – nothing evokes a blue sky quite like it.

When did *you* last glug yoghurt? In 2014, the Nutribullet brought liquidised kale to the fore. In that era, an unhappy man told me he drank green juices on weekdays and almond-milk-based drinks on weekends. Now we've entered the kefir years, and the supermarkets are devoting entire sections of their fridges to fermented milk. Drinking yoghurt is on the menu. In India it never left the menu, of course. Salty lassis come with a touch of cumin and sweet ones come frothy and creamy with a whisper of cardamom, flavoured with mango or papaya or avocado.

With all this in mind, I did some blitzing. Some of my favourite yoghurt drinks are coming up but I could've carried on forever. You'll find these things really come into their own after a bit of exercise, over ice, in the spring sunshine. My dad was on to something.

These all make two little ones. Just put everything into the blender and blitz (you'll need a powerful blender for the dates). Of course you can use your favourite plant-based yoghurt for these (ideally not coconut-based). Add a handful of ice cubes if you like, too.

Strawberry and rose
180g strawberries
220g plain yoghurt
2 tablespoons milk
1 tablespoon honey
½ teaspoon rose water

Orange blossom

the juice of 4 oranges
220g plain yoghurt
1½ tablespoons honey
¾ teaspoon orange blossom water

Apple-cinnamon

1 green apple, cored and chopped into chunks
220g plain yoghurt
5 tablespoons milk
2 tablespoons brown sugar
½ teaspoon cinnamon

Melon and cardamom

200g cantaloupe, chopped into chunks
220g plain yoghurt
4 tablespoons milk
1 tablespoon honey
crushed seeds from 4 cardamom pods

Date and vanilla

6 pitted dates
300g plain yoghurt
½ teaspoon vanilla extract
8 tablespoons milk

A cold lolly and a chit-chat

In the early, foggy, who-am-I? days of motherhood, everyone told me it would get easier. That seemed far-fetched.

As I took various questionnaires and doctors scribbled notes about the appropriateness of my coat and my ability to maintain eye contact, I felt like they had me all wrong. It wasn't 'motherhood' I was finding hard; I was struggling to love and physically look after myself, not my daughter (though I did feel very sorry that she'd had to be born to me and not someone better). This new situation was throwing us so many curveballs that I'd had to put my own soul on hold while I did the requisite ducking and diving.

And time had taken on a whole new meaning. So it being easier in six months wasn't a comfort to me, because six months into the future wasn't a time I could consider. It was thousands of nappies and soggy muslins and who knows what else away. There would be too many appointments attended in body only, too many Wednesdays, too many forgotten teas, too many walks in the park watching other parents move normally, while they worried about normal things like sleep and teeth. I didn't feel like I would make it to six months, which sounds more morbid than I was aware of feeling, but I couldn't see that it was possible for me to keep being me for that long. I didn't believe I would ever be better, so my friend said that she would just believe it for me while I couldn't.

There was no moment that everything felt easier, obviously. The notable moments were the ones in which I felt worse. These usually happened on holidays, when the onslaught slowed, and I was able to stop and think about all the different bits of my head and body that felt broken so that I might eventually be in a position to address them one by one. On Mondello beach in Sicily we ate seafood risotto while the baby slept and we clinked rosato glasses and I was madly, abominably aware this was the kind of thing I'd love if I wasn't lying dormant on the inside. On Instagram this might've been called a 'parenting win', but in clinical psychology it was called something else. I felt much worse here than I did sitting in the same armchair in my living room, with my baby, under a comfort blanket of tears, milk and vomit.

I am choosing which bits to write down and which bits not to. I'm opting not to give you the details of those early days, even though part of me – the big annoying bit that seeks your validation, despite not knowing who you are – wants to list them out so that you might DM me and say, 'Wow, Laura! You had it rough!' But I'm not doing it, because the truth is that you can have a 'smooth delivery' or a 'straightfor-ward' newborn period and still – because of chemicals – feel like you'll never be fully alive again.

There were so many moments of joy in the dark, but if there was a moment you might've looked into my eyes and said, 'Oh look, this woman is completely alive,' this is it: my daughter is almost two, which means eating has become more like eating and less like a science experi-ment. There are no more capsules of frozen gloop, and she chews her bread instead of gumming it. She can sit in the garden and have an ice lolly that's not secretly made of bitter greens without the neighbours calling the social on me.

Over the last two years, in naptimes and other snatches, just as he has dedicated himself to his wife and daughter, Rich has somehow turned our garden into the kind of idyll that makes children and adults stop outside the front of our house and peer all the way through in wonderment.

Now, when Z wakes from her post-lunch nap, we head out there, by the banana leaves. I go to the freezer to get us both an ice lolly, and she tells me whether she'd like a watermelon one or a stripy one. She checks I'm getting one for myself, too, and offers her dad one even if he's 'talkin' colleagues'. She asks for help taking her little orange chair out to the deck, and asks me to bring my 'brown chair', too. We sit together in the sun, with our feet in the paddling pool, which has a sprinkler in the shape of a turtle and coral-shaped accessories to complement the tropical fruit parasol our friend Aimee found for us, and Rich's jubilant, jungly planting. Z asks me what Peggy's doing and if we can look for earwigs and ants and seeds and wiggly worms. She points out every fly she sees and says 'cheers, lovey' when she holds her lolly up to clink against mine. She mutters about butterflies – touching butterflies, chasing butterflies. She gives my leg a pat and rests her head against it. 'We're having a rocket cold lolly, aren't we?' she says. And we are. We completely are.

Mango smoothie ice lollies

The lollies I like to kick around with are the simplest of the lollies – orange ones, lemon ones and mango ones. But the supermarket's mango lollies are only 30% mango, which isn't really enough per cent for a lolly that you're enjoying on the basis of its simplicity. I wouldn't say I was scared of stabilisers, just that I have no idea what they are, and I'm not crazy about the idea of a plain mango lolly that's mostly made of stuff. So I did what always seemed like a pipe dream: I wrangled with my lolly moulds until I understood them (another simple thing they made too complicated) and designed these, my family's perfect sunny day companions – just mango purée, coconut yoghurt and a bit of lime. Sit back, dangle your feet in a bucket of water. You'll feel better (I know it, even if you don't).

Makes 6 (regular lolly-sized) lollies

350g Alphonso mango pulp (from a tin)
200g coconut yoghurt
juice of 1 lime

1. Combine all the ingredients in a bowl and whisk together until smooth.

2. Transfer the mix to your lolly moulds and put the sticks in.

3. Freeze for at least 5 hours.

4. Before you attempt to ease the lollies from their moulds, run them under a warm tap for a minute.

To add booze
Replace 50g of mango pulp with 75ml of rum or tequila.

Power slurping

Paris and Nicole were not the role models our parents wanted for us. But in 2003, season one of *The Simple Life* – in which Paris Hilton and Nicole Richie were sent to Arkansas to do new poorly paid jobs every day – was entertainment like we'd never known. The critics called it 'cavernously stupid' and 'punishingly tedious' – 'an adventure in pointlessness' – but the ratings spoke for themselves.

I'm not saying I was altogether comfortable with the show; I recall wincing when it felt like people's real jobs were being mocked. This was always the worst bit of *The X Factor*, too – when the talent show was presented as the only viable means of escape from a normal, fortunate life. But for the most part, *The Simple Life* was just silly ('*I want to do makeovers on the cows*'). Watching now, it's striking how few 'confessionals' there are compared to modern equivalents – Paris and Nicole are rarely seen on a sofa, telling the camera how much they've learned. Each 20-minute episode is made up of hectically spliced footage of two women being ridiculous. I can see why I enjoyed it.

I don't love the massive wealth gap that made it possible, but I did love watching Paris and Nicole petulantly apply lip gloss into their Mac compact mirrors in a backroom while their boss for the day summoned them back from their break. I had a weekend job in a department store, and while I was there I clung to those brief spells with my locker, my Nokia 3310 and my lipgloss – a little time remembering who I was outside of Watford's Harlequin Centre. Paris Hilton and I have little else in common but I'm pretty sure we were wearing the same gloss (Mac's Prrr; I still wear it). I couldn't afford to lose my job, but man, I would've loved the chutzpah to keep applying makeup while my boss was trying to talk to me.

I'm not sure how much I knew about Paris's sex tape at the time, and I definitely was not yet au fait with the way the press routinely spoke about women, but on looking up some old reviews I found some insights into the world I was teenaging in.

The AV Club announced: 'The Simple Life confirms that Richie and Hilton are every bit as spoiled, vacant, superficial, mean, manipulative, dim-witted, materialistic, naïve, and boy-crazy as their reputations suggest.'

And of course there was much analysis of Paris's appearance. A man in Entertainment Weekly wrote: 'See, little Paris? You can run all the way to Altus, but you can't run away from heartbreak. And we know you've got a heart because we can see it beating against your ribcage through your shirt? DEAR GOD WILL YOU EAT A CUPCAKE OR SOMETHING AND PUT ON SOME WEIGHT, ALREADY!'

Even the good ship Guardian used real, old-school column inches to speculate that a sex tape leaked without Paris's knowledge or consent was a publicity stunt: 'Hotel heiress "embarrassed" at scandal which conveniently coincides with launch of her TV show.' The writer added: 'those who have seen the tape describe it as average'.

And those are just the ones that are still online.

So, while on some level I definitely processed *The Simple Life* as an act of defiance, I didn't realise exactly what was going on. Paris and Nicole were trying to show that they'd remain on their bullshit in spite of what people wrote or thought about them. There was the gloss, the flip phone, the big sunglasses, and there was another prop that women 'living in the public eye' seemed to use to convey that they were living in spite of a gross invasion of their privacy: a drink with a straw. Looking back at pictures from the paparazzi's 'golden years' – especially of Britney – you can see that these women needed a slurpable crutch if they were going to step outside, straight into the lion's den. This was how, in the early noughties, you acted casual – you seemed sure of yourself, when you were not.

It was perhaps a problematic route to rebellion, but this is truly how I learned to begin to extricate myself from the things people thought about me, or the things I thought people thought about me. I used the props at my disposal, and for me the most liberating one was a highly-sweetened, iced, blended coffee drink made by an American multinational chain we now know doesn't pay its taxes.

I was a regular teen – the exact type you imagine would end up writing a book like this one – which means I could not find a comfortable way to exist. But when I started taking myself into town to do a dance class and drink a highly-sweetened, iced, blended coffee drink, I started to work it all out. I stopped waiting for anyone to be available to do the class I wanted to do. I just started going to do it. The feeling of freedom was so profound that I recognised it fluttering in my stomach immediately when – in 2021 – I went for my first solo potter in town after a baby and several lockdowns. Having spent a lot of time wondering what kind of world I'd brought my daughter into, I was so excited to think she has this feeling ahead of her.

And that's why I still think of slurping as a radical act of joy. Slurping a milkshake instead of silently sipping it is better than when you take your best stab at an ujjayi breath in a yoga class. The louder you slurp, the more yourself you feel.

Chocolate malt shake

For a time, I was obsessed with the idea of owning a Hamilton Beach Milkshake Maker – and, look, maybe I still am.

Google it and see how mad about California I really am. Even if you make it in a regular blender, as I sadly do, this particular slurpable tastes like the Pacific Coast Highway, wind in your hair, Ruffles in the glove compartment. A malt – or malted shake – is just a better milkshake, made thick and biscuity with malted milk powder. And you can easily make this vegan with chocolate sorbet (or any vegan chocolate ice cream), oat milk and vegan Horlicks. How fantastic? That we can easily drink excellent vegan malted milkshakes now. Hold my cup for a second; I want to feel the sea spray on my face.

Makes 1 big or 2 little ones

180g chocolate ice cream
140ml milk (any kind)
2½ tablespoons Horlicks

Blend, pour, slurp.

A 3 p.m. pina colada

The first sip of alcohol I ever had was my mum's Malibu and pineapple in the function room of a hotel in Cornwall which had a lot of ivy on the front and a pool table in the games room. The song was Kung Fu Fighting by Carl Douglas and some entertainment reps demonstrated how to kick on the beat. Wow, I thought, that's what being an adult is about – tropical milkshakes at the disco.

A little while after that, I was forced by my godforsaken peers to climb gates to drink alcohol in parks after they'd closed, and I'll never forget the pride on Daniel Peters's face when I 'calmly' downed a triple shot of sambuca, but I'll never drink sambuca again either. At university it was important to hold your own with triple vodka oranges on Wednesdays and triple vodka Red Bulls on Mondays. Other days, people drank snakebites, which were disgusting. Out of nowhere I noticed that wine was delicious, and by wine I mean White Zinfandel. Later, I realised that red wine was great to drink in France and you didn't have to do anything in triples to have a nice time, unless you wanted to. And later still, when life got real, as it does, I decided I like my wine funky and mossy with a touch of pig sty. I still don't like Negronis but am married to a fanatic. I went through a lot to get to where I am today, which is drinking a cocktail that is the best possible expression of Malibu and pineapple.

This is my favourite way to halt a day that is simply not working out. It may be just past lunchtime but we are not tackling our to-do lists any more and I can't make my meeting; it's just not feasible in the current climate, I hope you understand. The sun is shining, which is not nothing, so I'm heading into the garden to drink a pina colada. If my little dependent is kicking around, I'll drop the rum in the recipe below to make her a virgin version and let her go loopy with cocktail umbrellas. If anyone needs me, I'll be in a deckchair shirking my responsibilities for 20 glorious minutes. That's what being an adult is about.

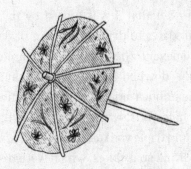

Makes one

100g caster sugar (for sugar syrup, optional, see step 1)
60ml white or golden rum
215g frozen pineapple (from a supermarket-bought bag, or
    fresh pineapple chopped and frozen yourself)
60g coconut milk, shaken
1 tablespoon lime juice
a splash of double cream, or vegan double cream
    (optional)

1. If you want to be able to control the sweetness, make a
    sugar syrup by dissolving 100g of caster sugar in 50ml
    of water over a low heat. Cool before using. I don't
    always do this, because the bagged frozen pineapple
    tends to be sweet enough for me, but a little sugar syrup
    is handy to have.

2. In a powerful blender, combine the rum, pineapple,
    coconut milk and lime. Taste and sweeten tentatively
    with syrup if you like.

3. Pour the frosty drink into your glass and, if you like, drizzle a little double cream and swirl it through with the back of a spoon.

4. Garnish garishly (maraschino cherry, umbrella, paper pineapple, flamingo swizzle stick, you get me).

How should a sherbet be?

I want to be wearing all different bits of jewellery on all different body parts – stacking rings and jangly bracelets and necklaces of compatible lengths, depending on the day and how I'm feeling. And I want to be out and about, secure in the knowledge that when my lips feel a bit dry I'll know how to resuscitate the lipstick I carefully (but with fluency and speed) applied earlier, and I will just have a sixth sense for when the colour might be about to fade. I will reapply the lipstick exactly then, not a minute later; that's just the kind of person I am. If I'm lucky enough to reach old age, I will waft around in zebra-print linen two-pieces and beautiful bejewelled earrings with the same perfect lips everyone has grown to expect of me.

In reality, I don't own enough pieces of jewellery that I might adorn myself according to my mood, and I don't have time in my schedule to determine my mood anyway. I have over-plucked eyebrows and scarred skin that doesn't look good with a lot of makeup on it, and doesn't look great without makeup either. I pick my lips when I'm stressed. I have absolutely no idea how to do hair, or what utensils I'd need if I wanted to try.

Sort of similarly, I wanted to give you a recipe for orange sherbet served in an orange half. But when it came to it, I didn't have the energy to scrape out all the pith, string, sponge and cobweb from inside the oranges in order to create an almost serviceable bowl, when I already own so many actual bowls (nice ones! Lovingly pursued on eBay!), and I didn't think the orange shells looked that nice anyway. I could not find the sense in what I was doing from the carnage on my worktop.

So I was going to tell you to be extra, to take your sherbet to town by serving it in this extravagant style, to let these oranges be their best, most flamboyant selves, to scoop like mad. But I ended up facing the reality of the person I am. Someone who needs to find the sense in absolutely everything. Someone who wore bottle green corduroy blazers as a punctual, studious 19-year-old. Someone who took trainers to their own wedding. Guess what? I loved it all. And the sherbet – like a frothier, fizzier, softer sorbet – tastes good, whatever you put it in.

Orange sherbet

Makes about 800ml

500ml orange juice
125ml lemon juice
200g sugar
⅛ teaspoon fine sea salt
170ml double cream (or any vegan alternative)

1. If you're using an ice cream maker, have your ice cream bowl well frozen, ideally for a day or two.

2. Have all the juice squeezed and ready to go in a big jug or bowl.

3. Take 250ml of your citrus juice and put it into a little saucepan with the sugar and salt. Heat it gently until the sugar has completely dissolved.

4. Add that back in with the rest of the juice and let it all cool in the fridge for a couple of hours.

5. Mix the (also cold) cream into the syrup, tip the mix straight into the ice cream maker and churn according to your machine's preferences. If you don't have a machine, transfer the mixture immediately to a big Tupperware in the freezer and take it out to give it a mix every 30 minutes for 2½ hours – this is not a fobbing off, it works perfectly.

6. When you're ready to serve, let the sherbet warm up for 5 minutes before scooping it into bowls. And remember: the way you serve your pudding is not a reflection of who you are.

LIFE SNACKS V (icons only)

- Flamin' Hot Cheetos.

(That's it.)

SNACKCETERA

If you're interested in getting into the condiment game, these are my favourite snack-enhancing extras to make. I didn't plan it this way but it turns out you need a lot of anchovies.

B2L green sauce

At some point in high lockdown I bought a magnetic note-pad for the outside of my fridge purely to tell me what was inside the fridge. Truly the system of an ignoramus, but I am an ignoramus and so it worked for me – I got much better than I'd previously been at using the food I'd bought (one of my life strategies is to periodically imagine describing something I'm doing to a caveperson. With this fridge list, I would struggle).

This sauce, inspired by all the chimichurris and salsa verdes that came before it, is a way to bring your languishing parsley and coriander back 2 life, back 2 reality. But it's also a way to hype them up, so they can permeate your existence for as long as they live.

The quantities I've given should be used as a rough guide only; just go with what you have. I use the stalks – I'm not sure of the correctness of this, but I like it. And feel free to chuck in a bit of dill or basil as your magnetic fridge note-pad dictates.

Stuff the ingredients into your NutriBullet while listening to Soul II Soul's Back To Life and enjoy a grim little trip down pandemic memory lane.

Good with: a toastie, a sausage, pizza crusts, roast chicken, hot new potatoes, a beany taco, scrambled egg.

Makes about 65g

handfuls of parsley and coriander, stalks and all
  (approx. 15g all-in)
½ clove of garlic
½ chilli (optional)
1 anchovy (or capers if vegetarian)
15ml red wine vinegar
45ml extra virgin olive oil
salt and pepper

1. Put everything except the oil into a blender or food processor and go for your life. Pulse if you prefer to keep it chunkier.

2. Stir through the oil and add salt and pepper to taste. (Adjust anything and everything else to taste, too!)

Mixed pickles

In our house, when we are at the straggliest ends of our wits and have no idea what to eat, these pickles sort us out. There's something about my chosen vegetable mix – the medley of colours and textures – that will turn an otherwise forlorn plate into something to get jazzed about. I want you to get jazzed, too, so make sure you choose the vegetables most likely to have that effect – radishes, beetroot, peppers and thinly sliced cabbage all pickle well, but you are the conductor of your own jazzy future.

Good with: cheese, hummus, salty crisps, egg mayo, leftover roast chicken, little ham baps, egg-fried rice, potato salad.

Makes enough for 2 big (i.e. Mrs Elswood pickle) jars

500g mixed vegetables. I like:
turnip (1)
cauliflower (somewhere between ¼ and ½)
cucumber (½)
carrots (2)

400ml cider vinegar
400ml water
1 tablespoon caster sugar
1 teaspoon salt
1 teaspoon black peppercorns
1 teaspoon mustard seeds
2 tablespoons chopped dill

1. Heat everything but the vegetables and dill in a pan until the sugar and salt have dissolved. Leave to cool.

2. Peel the turnip and carrots, and cut all the vegetables into bite-size pieces. I like the turnips in batons, the cauliflower in small florets, and the cucumber in spears. I cut the carrots into little angled chunks after slicing

them in half lengthways. None of this matters *exactly*; it's just that having a variety of shapes makes for a better eating experience.

3. Mix the vegetables up and arrange them across the two jars.

4. Split the dill across the jars, too.

5. Pour the cooled liquid over the vegetables, making sure they're all submerged. If they're not, add water.

6. Put the lids on the jars and leave to pickle in the fridge for 10 days. The pickles are good to eat for a month.

Kalamata and fig tapenade

I'm not going to pretend that tapenade is as handy to have in the fridge as some of the other items in this section – all the articles telling me to swirl it into my soups and stews can do one. But it is a paste of all the saltiest things, which means it couldn't be snackier and consequently it tends to do really well among a wider network of nibbles. Plus, the jars of tapenade you can buy for too many pounds are not as delicious or as abundant as this.

Good with: crostini, baguette, fish, leftover roast chicken, buttery corn on the cobs, fried eggs, goat's cheese (see pinwheels on page 187), feta (see baked feta on page 97), burrata, toasties.

Makes 300g

100g dried figs, stalks removed, chopped into quarters
100ml water
150g pitted Kalamata olives
2 teaspoons capers
1 anchovy
1 small clove of garlic, peeled
1 teaspoon fresh thyme leaves
1½ tablespoons lemon juice
70ml extra virgin olive oil

1. Put the chopped figs into a pan with 100ml of water on
    a medium heat and cook until there's no water left.

2. Put the now-sticky figs into a food processor with the
    olives, capers, anchovy, garlic, thyme and lemon juice
    and blitz to a rough purée. With the motor still run-
    ning, add the oil.

3. Or, pound all the solids in a pestle and mortar, then
    transfer it to a bowl and stir through the lemon juice
    and oil.

Caponata

I arrive in Paris at lunchtime and head straight to Chez
Aline because I know it will make me feel good about my
decisions without spoiling my dinner. It's a little lunchbox
of a place containing a deli counter and four bar stools.
Sandwiches are served in yellow plastic baskets; I've never

had the same sandwich twice, and I've never had a bad one either. There are snacks to have on the side, of which my favourites are oeufs mimosa (devilled eggs) and caponata.

Caponata is stewed, vinegary, slightly sweet aubergines, celery and onion with lots of pockets of fun (capers! Olives! Raisins!). It's Sicilian, not French, though it does particularly well mopped up with baguette.

Good with: a whole sandwich, a fried egg, mozzarella, crostini, socca, tinned tuna.

Serves 6–8 as a snack (obviously)

about a litre of vegetable, rapeseed or sunflower oil, for
    deep-frying
2 aubergines (about 600g), cut into 2–3cm dice
3 tablespoons olive oil
2 small red onions, finely sliced
3 sticks of celery, in 1cm slices
salt and pepper
½ teaspoon chilli flakes
1 x 400g tin of chopped tomatoes
60ml red wine vinegar
1 tablespoon honey
10 green olives, pitted and roughly chopped
2 tablespoons capers
1½ tablespoons raisins
about 4 tablespoons roughly chopped parsley
40g flaked almonds, toasted in a dry frying pan

1. Roll your sleeves up for a spot of deep-frying. Pour your frying oil into a deep pan so that it comes 5–8cm up the sides and the pan is no more than a third full.

2. Heat the oil to 190°C. If you don't have a thermometer, use a cube of bread – if it's crisp and golden within 30 seconds you're good to go.

3. Fry the aubergines in three batches, re-establishing the 190°C frying temperature in between. Let the cubes of aubergine bob around in the oil, prodding them intermittently with a spider strainer until they're golden all over (3–5 minutes depending on how everything's doing). Rest the fried cubes on plenty of kitchen paper.

4. Put the olive oil into a wide pan with a lid, and when it's hot, cook the onions and celery with a pinch of salt over a medium heat until soft.

5. Add the chilli flakes, stir, and cook for another minute.

6. Add to the pan: tinned tomatoes, fried aubergine, red wine vinegar, honey, olives, capers, raisins and several twists of black pepper. Rinse the tomato can with a little water and slosh that in too.

7. Stir well, put the lid on, and leave it to simmer for 30 minutes.

8. Let the caponata come to room temperature and check the seasoning before scattering with parsley and almonds to serve.

Mayonnaise

To leave this out would be, for me, like going to dinner without hoops in my ears. I don't need to tell you how to use it.

Good with: your life.

Makes about 225g

2 teaspoons Dijon mustard
2 egg yolks
salt and pepper
200ml groundnut oil
25ml extra virgin olive oil
1 tablespoon white wine vinegar
1 teaspoon lemon juice

1. Rest a bowl on a folded tea towel to stop it moving when you start whisking.

2. Put the mustard, egg yolks and a pinch of salt into the bowl, and whisk to combine.

3. Begin to dribble in the groundnut oil, whisking all the while. Start with droplets and build up to a slow trickle. Don't stop whisking.

4. Do the same with the olive oil.

5. Whisk through the vinegar, lemon juice and add salt and pepper to taste.

Aïoli

For a dipping aïoli, you can just add a crushed or minced garlic clove or two to the mayonnaise. But if you need something sturdier and more pungent, closer to the original aïoli, for spreading on toast (like for the sardine party on page 171), let me tell you what I would do (though I can't tell you how much garlic you can handle). This'll make about 180g.

I would crush 3 cloves of garlic in a pestle and mortar, with a big pinch of salt. I'm normally a fan of mincing via Microplane, but for this it only tastes right after a pounding. Then I would move away from the pestle and mortar because I can't really be doing with sloshy yolks and oil in this bath-like tool that's literally from the Stone Age. So I'd use a spatula to scrape every last morsel of the pounded garlic into a bowl where it would meet 2 egg yolks, and then I would continuously drizzle and whisk 180ml of oil (either a mix of groundnut and extra virgin, or just regular olive). And I'd squeeze half a lemon straight in, for the faintest relief, just to undo the top button.

YOU ARE NOW LEAVING SNACKTOWN

You've slurped your milkshake to its crescendo and the open road is stretching into the sky ahead of you; adjust your sun shield and reach for the glove compartment – you probably stashed something good in there, under the de-icer. Or maybe you didn't. With any luck, there are many more snacks ahead of you. In fact, once you've put this book down, it'll only be seconds, minutes, an hour before it's time for the next one.

I can't speak for you (you can, in your Amazon review) but I've loved the chance to examine our snackiest moments. I'm the sort of person who spends hours that would be better spent watching TV or reading a book just churning through thoughts, so it's likely I'd have meditated on a donut anyway, but now I will really notice my donuts. I think I will even notice my hummuses.

After writing this, I will be much more inclined, if I'm lucky enough to go to America again, to see the Cheez-Its in my trolley for what they've always been: a core part of my experience. Not a red box I could easily do without. I'll pause longer in holiday supermarkets to make sure I've taken it all in, and I'll learn to switch off the voice in my head that tells me the mustard Lay's aren't worth it – I'll ruin my dinner. You can't ruin anything with joy.

I'll provide snacks when people are coming over regardless of whether it's 'really necessary'. But if I'm not up to it, I won't.

I will not resent my daughter's third request of the day for crisps, but I will reject it.

As for coffee. If you love it like I do, you might be familiar with the deeply decentring feeling of being 'off it' – through illness or pregnancy or feelings. I was completely off it while I finished writing this book and I cannot wait for the moment I wake from this nauseous slumber. The music will be loud, the coffee pot will be hotter than the experts would like it to be, and the cherry pies will – like me – be their best selves again. Like the first snowdrops of spring, but with cream cheese cake.

Safe travels, then. Thanks for swinging by. Turn the stereo up and dance like no one's watching. Drink each coffee like you'll feel too sick tomorrow. Snack your heart out.

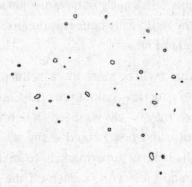

ACKNOWLEDGEMENTS

Writing this book was a quiet experience, quieter than writing CARBS. More in my head, pieced together in scraps of time – and I send so much love and gratitude to the people who provide sanity every day in my WhatsApps like it's nothing: Laura Goulden, Janet Oliver, Annie Barber, Rosie Manning, Claudia Phillips, Joanna Packman, Marie-Claire Amuah, Ian Chaloner, Tillie Peacock, Aimee Phillips and Jean Edelstein all make time for a lot of chaotic white speech bubbles. And also my dog, Peggy, who doesn't respond to my texts, but soothes like no human can.

With special thanks to Janet whose elite service has provided much snack intel for this book.

I am grateful to good people at my day job, especially Katherine Wilkin, whose flexibility and understanding helped keep me afloat through lockdowns, pregnancies, babies and a book.

Thanks to my agent, Sabhbh Curran, for stepping up and cracking on with the energy I needed in 2021 when there wasn't even much energy in the world. As well as my editor,

Anna Steadman, whose calm, thoughtful notes made this book better than it was going to be.

Thank you to Daisy Parente for believing from the beginning, and to Susannah Otter for being an ear and a light. And everyone who supported CARBS in all the ways – by buying it for your people, cooking from it, talking about it and loving it.

I am wildly grateful to the people who keep my household ticking along – my parents-in-law, Pawsome Pals, Albert's, Rosie and Jamie, and especially our beloved childminder, Ann-Marie.

Thank you to my family for the jokes and the food; imagine this book without those two things. Imagine me without those two things!

I want to thank Zip, whose snacking prowess, cracking sense of humour, chatter, twirling and chutzpah inspire me endlessly.

And actually there are not enough thanks in the world for Rich who tells me 'we'll work it out' when it seems impossible. I'm thankful we get to work it out together every day, with snacks and so much laughter.

ENDNOTES

WELCOME TO SNACKTOWN

The Hartman Group (2017), 'Snacking: The Great Change Agent Disrupting Food Culture', *Forbes* magazine, 16 May.

Wilson, Bee (2019), 'Let's Bring Back the Proper Snack', *Wall Street Journal,* 5 September.

FOREVER FAVES

Beggs, Alex (2020), 'There's an Entire Industry Dedicated to Making Foods Crispy, and It Is WILD', *Bon Appetit,* 20 February.

Tunick, Michael (2013), 'Critical Evaluation of Crispy and Crunchy Textures: A Review', *International Journal of Food Properties,* 2 April.

By The Glass (2018), 'Professor Charles Spence on the science behind crispy chips', *Adelaide Review,* 23 January.

Spence, Charles (2017), *Gastrophysics: The New Science of Eating,* Viking.

Szczesniak, Alina (1991), 'Textural Perceptions and Food Quality', *Journal of Food Quality,* February.

Perelman, Deb (2016), 'The Consummate Chocolate Chip Cookie, Revisited', *smittenkitchen.com*, 3 June.

DIPS

Hayden, Georgina (2019), *Taverna*, Square Peg.

CARBY THINGS

George, Tonia (2009), *Things on Toast*, Ebury Publishing.

The Serenity Now, *Seinfeld*, Larry David, Jerry Seinfeld, Steve Koren, Season 9, Episode 3; 1997. Produced by Shapiro/West Productions with Castle Rock Entertainment.

Dream Job, *Peep Show*, Jesse Armstrong, Sam Bain, Andrew O'Connor, Season 1, Episode 5; 2003. Produced by Objective Productions.

Instagram.com/drbeckyatgoodinside.

CHEESY THINGS

Saxelby, Anne (2020), *The New Rules of Cheese*, Ten Speed Press.

Roux, Michel (2017), *Cheese*, Quadrille Publishing Ltd.

Our Cup Runneth Over, *Schitts Creek*, Dan Levy, Eugene Levy, Chris Pozzebon, Season 1, Episode 1; 2015. Produced by Canadian Broadcasting Corporation with Not A Real Company.

The Drip, *Schitts Creek*, Dan Levy, Eugene Levy, Chris Pozzebon, Season 1, Episode 2; 2015. Produced by Canadian Broadcasting Corporation with Not A Real Company.

Buffardi, Michelle (2013), *Great Balls of Cheese*, Houghton Mifflin Harcourt.

Lattin, Clare and Hill, Tom (2016), *Ducksoup Cookbook: The Wisdom of Simple Cooking,* Square Peg.

Hopkinson, Simon, 'Parmesan biscuits', *bbc.co.uk.*

A CUP OF COFFEE

The Suicide, *Seinfeld,* Larry David, Jerry Seinfeld, Tom Leopold, Season 3, Episode 15; 1992. Produced by Shapiro/West Productions with Castle Rock Entertainment.

Jones, Evan (1975), *American Food: The Gastronomic Story,* Random House.

Smith, Delia, 'Good Old Rock Cakes', *deliaonline.com.*

Al Kasimi, Alia, Cookingwithalia.com (original recipe no longer online).

Episodes #1.1 and #1.3, *Twin Peaks,* Mark Frost, David Lynch, Harley Peyton; 1990. Produced by Propaganda Films, Spelling Entertainment and Lynch/Frost Productions.

Barrow, Cathy (2019), *When Pies Fly,* Grand Central Publishing (Hachette Book Group).

Elsen, Emily and Elsen, Melissa (2013), *The Four & Twenty Blackbirds Pie Book,* Grand Central Life & Style (Hachette Book Group).

Steinberg, Sally Levitt (2004), *The Donut Book,* Storey Publishing.

A GLASS OF WINE

Willan, Anne (1981), *French Regional Cooking,* Hutchinson & Co.

Grigson, Jane (1967), *Charcuterie and French Pork Cookery,* Michael Joseph.

SNACKS ON ICE

Sawyer, Terry (2003), 'The Simple Life', Pop Matters, 8 December.

Shales, Tom (2003), 'How Low Will Fox Stoop? Here's a Simple Answer', Washington Post, 2 December.

Rabin, Nathan (2004), 'The Simple Life', AV Club, 10 February.

Wolk, Josh (2003), 'The girls' hands go where the sun don't shine', *Entertainment Weekly,* 17 December.

Luscombe, Richard (2003), 'Sex video gives Paris Hilton publicity money can't buy', *Guardian*, 7 December.

INDEX

Laura Goodman is a food writer whose work has appeared in the *Sunday Times, Eater, Food52, Lucky Peach* and *Waitrose Magazine*. From January 2019 to January 2020 she wrote a weekly column about snacks for *Grazia*. Her first cookbook, *Carbs*, was published by Quadrille in 2018. Nigella Lawson called it 'wonderful', Meera Sodha called it 'joyful, funny and intelligent' and Rukmini Iyer called it her 'favourite cookbook'. @laurajgood